Advance Praise for *Beyond Shatt*

"This collection is a document that refuses the idea of collateral damage ... [It] is filled with humanity, laden with stories of love, tragic loss, days of survival, and death ... *Beyond Shattered Glass* is ultimately a work of altruism and resistance ... The words give voice to traces which are not made of stones, but of lasting voices of love and condemnation."

—**Rawi Hage, *author of* Beirut Hellfire Society *and* De Niro's Game**

"Great tragedies in history often generate one epic moment that fully encapsulates the pain, the rage, and the absurdity of it all. The Beirut explosion was, undoubtedly, such an event. Decades of war and destruction, so many lives broken and wasted, a nation humiliated and plundered by those who were supposed to protect it. And suddenly, in a single blast, everything is shattered, everything is exposed, everything is revealed. On that fateful day in August, the authors of this book obviously suffered; they wept; they tried to comfort their loved ones; then they wiped their tears and began to write. Their testimony is powerful, as literature can be powerful when it discards all that is futile to focus on what is humanly essential."

—**Amin Maalouf, *author of* Samarkand *and* The Gardens of Light**

"This prismatic, gripping book is unforgettable. Its writers offer truth, love, and action in place of untruths and impunity. Out of so many fragments, through so many entangled lives, these memories create another kind of city, a place where belonging and dignity are offered, held, and lived."

—**Madeleine Thien, *novelist and short story writer***

"Faced with a barbaric obscenity that mutilated indiscriminately, we realized that the executioners are still among us: Those who know but do not speak; those who speak but do not act; and those who continue to obstruct the investigations of the Beirut Port blast, assassinating the victims and their families for a second time. When the world no longer made sense, when our breath carried neither our words nor the soul of our dead, there remained our naked, living, raw humanity whispering to us: 'You, the living, this is what bonds us to you, to this life, and to what we have been.' These stories of shattered glass, of shredded hopes, and of sacrificial love are the voices of the voiceless. They are brought to you here as a sacred offering to keep their memories alive."

—*Zena Wakim, international lawyer, and Jayce Salloum, artist and filmmaker*

"*Beyond Shattered Glass* is a collection of necessary voices that unflinchingly show us what it's like to be broken and human in the aftermath of one of modern history's most devastating explosions. It's a love letter by and for the survivors and the grief-stricken, the inhabitants of a harsh, beloved, wounding, and wounded city."

—*Zeina Hashem Beck, author of* O *and* Louder than Hearts

"It is insufficient to describe the stories in *Beyond Shattered Glass* as heartbreaking or tragic. These powerful, intimate acts of witness to the Beirut explosion are much more than that. Detailed and unflinching, they are an indictment of government incompetence and corruption, as well as a centering of those who paid an incalculable price for it. What emerges is a portrait of modern Lebanon in all its beauty and brokenness, a kaleidoscope of life on either side of calamity. This is morally and historically vital work."

—*Omar El Akkad, novelist and journalist*

"An urgent and unique document which provides a complex tapestry of humanity pushed to extremes. This event shows the best and worst in our collective condition, and this book is a beautiful account of these unforgettable journeys."

—*Atom Egoyan, film director*

VOICES
FROM THE AFTERMATH
OF THE BEIRUT
EXPLOSION

beyond shattered glass

COLLECTED
& INTRODUCED
BY ZEINA SAAB

EDITED BY
RL ATTIEH
& NADIA TABBARA

FOREWORD BY RAWI HAGE

OLIVE
BRANCH
PRESS

An imprint of Interlink Publishing Group, Inc.
Northampton, Massachusetts

First published in 2023 by

Olive Branch Press
An imprint of Interlink Publishing Group, Inc.
46 Crosby Street, Northampton, MA 01060
www.interlinkbooks.com

Library of Congress Cataloging-in-Publication data:
ISBN-13: 978-1-62371-747-6

Printed and bound in the United States of America

*Dedicated to all those who senselessly lost their lives
due to the crime of August 4.*

May they rest in peace. And may justice be served.

Abbas Ahmed Mazloum
Abdel Halim El Ali Salem
Abdel Kader Bloso
Abdul-Muhib Mikhlif Al-Aziz
   Al-Murshidani
Abdel Rahman Bshenati
Abdo Tanious Ata
Abdul Kader Ali Terras
Ahmad Ibrahim Kaadan
Ahmad Mohammad Omeira
Alexandra Naggear
Ali Abbas Ismail
Ali Abdo Ayoub
Ali Hussein Zeineddine
Ali Ibrahim Jassem Obeid
Ali Ismail El Sayed Chahata

Ali Kassem Sawan
Ali Mehsen Mcheik
Alice Balian
Amer Hussein
Amin Zahed
Amina Salim Karbik
Anette Karabit Khatchikian
Antoine Bassil
Antoine Flouty
Antoine Zaarour
Antoine Barmaki
Aram Ter-Sarkissian
Ardel Maglangit
Arlette Jean Kattah
Armand Tayan
Asmahan Sarouf Bou Rjeily

Ayman Assem Suleiman
Ayman Mostapha al Homsi
Ayman Noureddine
Ayman Obeid
Ayoub Jouni
Azadoui Malkoun
Azam Yehya Hamawi
Babylynn Serohijos
Bissan Tibati
Cedra Al Kenno
Chakeh Sadek
Chadi Abi Chakra
Chant Hagopian
Charbel Abdo Matta
Charbel Hitti
Charbel Karam
Chawki Mohammad Allouch
Chawki Merheb
Claudette El Halabi
Claudia Lakkis
Cyril Michel Kanaan
Delia Guedikian Papazian
Diana (Anahid) Wahram Papazian
Diana Khoury
Dima Abdel Samad Kaiss
Dolly Kassem Khoury
Elias Bassam Khoury
Elie Khouzami
Elie Nouhad Nawfal
Ensaf Attar
Estephan Said Rouhanna
Etanu Dechassa Tullu
Fadi Hussein Al-Rabih
Fares George Kiwan
Farida Khoury Ghosn

Farouk Al Sallou
Fawzi Koleilat
Feryal Al Kiki
Firas Dahwish
Gabrielle Brigitte Kuhnle-Radtke
Gaia Fadoulian
Gerges Farjallah Daibes
Georges Haddad
Georges Maalouf
Georges Naja Freiha
Georges Pierro Demiani
Georges Saad
Georges Salim Al Wez
Georges Madi
Ghassan Hasrouty
Gretta Atallah Khoury
Hadi Succar
Hadi Assaf
Hala Sabbagh Tayyah
Hamad Medhat Al Attar
Hamza Hussein Iskandar
Hanna Gerges Akabatii
Hassan Moustapha Tay
Hassan Akram Chames
Hassan Ali Maneh
Hassan Kamel Haidar
Hassan Sadek
Hawlo Ahmad Abbas
Hayat Gergi Fadel
Hayle Mariam Dimisi Rita
Hedwig Waltmans-Moliere
Houssam Batal
Hussein Abd El Rahim Besher
Ibrahim Amin
Ibrahim Harb

Ibrahim Kaffas

Imad Zahreddine

Isaac Oehlers

Issa Khodor

Iyad Al Amin

Isabelle Machaalani

Jacqueline Gebrine

Jacques Gemayel

Jacques Sarkis Paramakian

Jad Gergeh Al Dahdah

Jad Samaha

Jamal Dod Miah

Jawad Ajwad Chaya

Jean Frederic Alam

Jean Marc Bonfils

Jean Said Kawbali

Jean Said Nehme

Jessica Bazidjian

Jessy Kahwaji Daoud

Jihad Antoine Saadeh

Jihad Omar

Joe Akiki

Joe Bou Saab

Joe Francis Haddad

Joe George Andoun

Joe Noun

Joseph Latif Merhi

Joseph Tanios Roukoz

Josephine Abou Zeid

Joud Hajj Steif Moustapha

Juliette Saab Aoude

Kaisar Fouad Abo Merhej

Kamal Kafa

Kassem Youssef Al Mawla

Kazem Chamseddine

Khaldiye Saaid Bakri

Khaled Wahoud

Khalil Badih Aoun Moujaes

Khalil Issa

Khodor Chafiq Badr

Kousay Fadi Ramadan

Krystel El Adm

Latifa Hajj Steif Moustapha

Laurette Owaida Richa

Lena Najjar Khazen

Leila Mitri Khoury

Lina Abo Hamdan

Lisa Hagop Kawoukjian

Mahmoud Ali Saiid

Mahmoud Hussein Khaled

Majida Saadeh Kassab

Malak Bazaza Ayoub

Margot Salim Tabbal

Maria-Pia Abo Sleiman

Marie Saad

Marion Hochar Ibrahimchah

Marie Farhat

Marie Khalil Tawk

Marine Elias

Mazen Raja Zwayhed

Mehdy Hassan Rami

Minerva Chartouni

Mireille Germanos

Misal Hawa

Mizan Jahangian Kha

Mohammad Ahmad Abbas

Mohammad Ahmad Ayrout

Mohammad Alaa Din

Mohammad Ali Abbas

Mohammad Damaj

Mohammad Hussein Al Sibaai

Mohammad Hussein Dgheim

Mohammad Issa Hammoud

Mohammad Ladiki

Mohammad Nour Doughan

Mohammad Obeid Hussein

Mohammad Sleiby

Mohammad Tleis

Mostapha Mohammad Ayrout

Nabil Suleiman

Nadia Bachir

Najat Haber Zeidan

Najib Hitti

Nawal Attieh

Nawal Hamdan

Nazar Najarian

Neamathallah Antoine Mekheiber

Nicolas Youssif Chedid

Nicole Majid Helou

Paulette Iskandar Hashem

Perlita Mendoza

Rabih Riyad Faraj

Ralph Mallahi

Rami Kaaki

Randa Elias Rizkallah

Rassil Massoud Mia

Rashed Hafizur

Rawan Misto

Rezol Mounir Sikda

Rita Antoine Hardini

Robert Youssef Semaan

Rushdi Al Jamal

Sabah Merhej Nassour

Sahar Fares

Salma Hatouni

Samir Boulous Karam

Sarkis Tekeryan

Sophie Khosrovian

Tanios Antoun

Tanios Mekhayel El Murr

Tharwat Hoteit

Therese Ghandour Merhi

Therese Khoury

Varoujan Tussonian

Wahib Abi Aad

William Azar

Wissam Faisal

Youssef Saleh Lahoud

Yvette Gergi Al Mini

Yvonne Sursock (Lady Cochrane)

Zahwa Dada

Zeina Chamoun

Zeina Ramzi Raji Zaarour

Zeinat Mougharbel Abbas

Zeid Mayta

Ziad Mostafa Al Sobh

Zoulbab Sajid Ali

To learn about the victims, please visit beirut607.org/alive-ashes/

CONTENTS

ACKNOWLEDGMENTS

Our deepest thanks to everyone who contributed their personal accounts to this book. You recalled, retold, and relived these tragic events because you knew how important it is to document our respective histories. Thank you for your trust.

To the fearless writers who poured their hearts into this project and persevered despite the many challenges: you cared so deeply, and it shows in every word of these adaptations.

Many thanks as well to those who provided support, guidance, and feedback along the way: Niamh Fleming-Farrell, Jasmina Najjar, Rawi Hage, Zena el Khalil, Mayda Freij-Makdissi, Ali Chehadeh, Ronnie Chatah, Maghie Gali, Mekdas Wedaje, Zahra Hankir, Loulya Halwany, Sophia Kagan, Bassam Jalgha, Munir David Nabti, Patricia Nabti, Samar Hammam, Faysal Saab, Sara Sibai, Hilda Abla, Reem Saab, Yasmine Dagher, Carol Ammoun, our legal team over at Capital Law Practice, Chris Abi Saab, Jessica Matta, and Michel Freifer, and of course, our incredible publisher, Interlink and specifically Michel Moushabeck, for his invaluable guidance and for understanding the importance of publishing such a book.

The following individuals helped connect us to contributors to ensure we collected a wide variety of stories, though we know there are so many more to tell: Farah Salka, Anamê Gnanguenon, Mona Hallak, Dima Safwan, Mark Darido, Nathaly Gattas, Wael Ghawi, Jessica Said Tabarly, Diane Assaf, Karim Kattouf, Myrna Abi Abdallah-Doumit, and the Order of Nurses in Lebanon.

This book wouldn't have been possible without the support of every single person who contributed to the Indiegogo crowdfunding efforts, where we raised money to fund the writing, editing, and design of this book. We wish we could list all the names here, but you can find them all on our website at www.bsgbeirut.com.

To Laila Kobrossy, Said Francis, Layal Nawfal, Myrna Atalla, Renée Codsi, Wassim and Maggie Kaiss, Ghaleb and Dida Saab, Manal and Ghassan Saab, Bassam Kassab and Maged Salib, Manuel and Stephanie Celedon, Lia Wadih, Michel and Gisèle Zovighian, Lynn and Paul Zovighian, and the Zovighian Partnership Team—your generosity touched us deeply and gave strong momentum to the campaign, allowing us to reach our fundraising goal in just ten days. Thank you all for your support.

FOREWORD

A few weeks after the Beirut explosion, a Lebanese government official declared in a televised newscast that the victims of the explosions had met "an unfortunate fate" (*Qada' wa Qadar*).

This dismissive statement baffled many of the victims, their families, and the rest of the nation. But it's not surprising that a government that, for the last four decades, has orchestrated a path of corruption and despotic rule, would have such an apathetic reaction. And now these rulers are seeking to eradicate all memories of the explosion. The government is eyeing the columns of grain silos that shielded multiple neighborhoods from the blast and intends to demolish them and remove them from the landscape.

The oligarchs who caused at least 228 to die, 7,000 to be injured, 300,000 to be displaced, and 77,000 homes and businesses to be destroyed, will never explain the clientelism, nepotism, violence, and long chain of incompetence and thefts that characterize them. They will never admit guilt. Instead, they will do everything in their power to block investigations and escape accountability. The veil is opaque.

The voices of those who were there and who are telling their stories have a denunciatory power and far-reaching agency. They witness, record, remember, and condemn.

This collection is a document that refuses the idea of collateral damage or "fate." It is a recitation that will endure, which does not look away from crimes and their aftermath, and which is filled with humanity, laden with stories of love, tragic loss, days of survival, and death.

These stories defy the cynical use of providence and all those who dismiss the innocents' calamity as an expression of fate. There is the story of a nurse who saves three infants born prematurely, and an injured Syrian worker seeking to reunite with his family. There are city streets covered in broken glass, young people carrying brooms and roaming the streets in order to help, people looking for their lost children. There are testimonies of artists, workers, neighbors, passengers and passersby, of local and transitory lives.

Beyond Shattered Glass is ultimately a work of altruism and resistance. It is a record of values and a collection of memories that stand against the immorality of power and imposed oblivion.

This government might succeed in eradicating the silos at the port, a massive monument embodying their failures and crimes. But these accounts by witnesses are another kind of remembrance and transformation. These words give voice to traces not made of stone but of lasting voices of love and condemnation.

—Rawi Hage, February 2023

INTRODUCTION

It must have been around three or four in the morning. I couldn't sleep. Hours earlier, one of the most powerful non-nuclear explosions in history had decimated a large part of my beloved capital city. I lay in bed, eyes wide open, heartbroken and terrified at our sudden new reality and bleeding world outside. I looked at my husband, who had succumbed to exhaustion moments earlier. I could have just as easily lost him.

Thousands of others had not been so lucky. The horror and shock of those first few hours quickly transformed into an avalanche of grief as news of the whereabouts of my relatives and friends began to pour in. Some were still missing, and the death toll was rising fast. I remember that in between my sobbing, I asked the walls around me, "Why?" Every passing second ached. Darkness engulfed me and I desperately wanted to wake up, but I knew we had all entered a new reality that we couldn't undo. Our Beirut, and the people in it, would never be the same.

I tried to imagine what our lives would be like moving forward. We were already living through a financial and economic meltdown, soaring unemployment rates, the collapse of the local currency, hyperinflation, political and governmental decay, and a pandemic. After the explosion on August 4th, how could we muster the strength to keep going?

Over the following days, it became clear what had happened: 2,750 tons of ammonium nitrate had been neglected by the Lebanese government since 2014 and dangerously stored at the Beirut port, in a heavily populated residential, commercial, and touristic area. Somehow, the chemicals had exploded, and as a result, at least 228 people were killed, at least 7,000 injured, several of whom have died from their injuries over the past couple of years, 77,000 homes and businesses damaged or destroyed, and 300,000 people displaced.

For a tiny country of six million, this was all just too much.

The revolution of October 17 had begun just a year earlier, in 2019, with hundreds of thousands of Lebanese taking to the streets for the first time in history to demand the removal of the entire political class who had thrived on corruption and abuse of power for well over thirty years. I marched in the streets of Gemmayze with hundreds of others, chanting and singing for the overthrow of the corrupt regime. The atmosphere was festive and full of hope. At one point, the crowd began to shout out a popular revolutionary chant in Arabic that translates to "All of you standing on your balconies, come down and join your people!" We were greeted with waves, smiles, and applause from the dozens of residents watching us from above.

These revolutionaries were fighting for better governance, and to ensure that the rule of law finally prevailed in Lebanon. On the day of the explosion, we would all learn exactly why what we were protesting for was so critical—corruption, conflict of interest, lack of accountability, and lack of transparency were all to blame for this catastrophe.

Just a few days after August 4, I marched again with hundreds of people on that same street, only this time, it was a candlelight vigil for the fallen. This time, the atmosphere was solemn. This time, there was no singing and the buildings around us were damaged or destroyed. And this time, when I looked up at the balconies, not a single person was standing there to greet us.

A month later, it was still difficult to get out of bed, but I managed to make it to ground zero to pay my respects to those who lost their lives. I attended a candlelight vigil on the same street that was once filled with crowded restaurants and bars. Now, it was an eerily dark, quiet ghost town, a place of mourning.

In the following weeks, although the people were still displaced, homes were still shattered, and hearts and bodies still broken, the dust had settled, and the streets had, in a way, cleared. And to my surprise, even the Souk el-Tayeb farmers market had opened in Mar Mikhael, effectively the central point of the blast. It was bustling with people greeting the villagers selling their authentic and locally made products: Arabic soap, spices, honey, chocolates, nuts, dried fruit, olives. Despite it all, signs of life were returning. Beirut refused to die.

It was there that I ran into an old friend of mine, Angelique, who was sitting with a man named Elias. They seemed to be old friends, but it turned out that they had met as a result of the explosion. Their story (which you can read about in this book) was remarkable. I began to wonder, what other stories were out there that showed the solidarity and support that emerged in the aftermath of the explosion, which is how the idea for this book transpired.

In the months that followed, I connected with contributors from all over the city and began to collect their testimonials in writing. It would take me a few more months after that to muster the courage to read them, and a painful few days of remembering and reflecting. Afterward, I felt the slight pang of catharsis and realized that sharing these stories could help. But they were so much more. They were stories of hope, solidarity, strength within the gaping hole of heartbreak and loss. This should never be forgotten.

After reading the drafts, I teamed up with Nadia Tabbara and RL Attieh for their guidance and support. Once we discussed and reviewed the testimonials from those affected by the explosion, we decided to pair them up with Lebanese writers, writers who live in Lebanon, or writers that have a strong connection to the country.

It was from this shared understanding that the writers reached out to the contributors, learned their stories intimately, and worked together to ensure that the stories are accurate to the experience of the contributors, emotionally and literally. The process was a collective one. It was a way to grieve together, and, above all, it was a way for the writers to lend their skills and expertise to give shape to these important stories and help them reach a wide audience.

These stories are meant to transport the reader to the place and time of August 4, 2020, in Beirut. They have been carefully selected to ensure a wide representation of Beirut's diverse social fabric—Lebanese, Lebanese-Armenian,

Syrians, Palestinians, Filipinas, Ethiopians, expatriates, and residents and citizens from various religious and socioeconomic backgrounds and neighborhoods.

In this book, we tell stories of survival—of a domestic worker's path towards rehabilitation after waking up from a coma; of the struggles of a laborer and the ultimate price he pays for trying to rescue a stranger. We tell stories of strength—how a nanny uses her quick thinking to save two little girls; how a yogi musters up her inner strength to find urgent support for her injured friend. We tell stories of solidarity—how a civil defense worker rushes to rescue people trapped in the rubble; how a young expat thousands of kilometers away sets up an online platform to help locate missing loved ones. We also honor the many who did not make it.

Through these stories, we pay tribute to the victims of the blast and continue to resist the unjust system of corruption and negligence that caused it. We are documenting, reading, and talking about real experiences, no matter how difficult they may be, in order to spread these stories to thousands more—a powerful form of nonviolent action and resistance.

Gradually, over weeks and months, life returned back to Beirut as life tends to do. Glass was swept up, businesses were renovated, people started to go out to restaurants and bars in Gemmayze and Mar Mikhael, and tourists returned. The massive destruction had all but been erased, only a few scars left behind. Amid crowds of people and the usual weekend traffic jams, the liveliness and bustle of Beirut was back.

Destroyed neighborhoods were now vibrant again, but it is always difficult to reconcile this with the tragedy that we had experienced. Our anger is still on the surface and our pain runs deep, yet it felt as if it had been covered by a fresh coat of paint.

It has been nearly three years now and we still don't have any accountability for this crime. Investigations have been stalled and obstructed by powerful political parties. As a result, we have no conclusive proof about who brought the ammonium nitrate into the port; nothing about why it was dangerously stored there for years; nothing about who was responsible for it; nothing about how and why it exploded. Instead, the Lebanese government simply covers up for itself.

While no book could ever give justice to all the lives lost and destroyed, forgetting this crime and moving on would be equally tragic. We must never accept what happened. We must never forget those who perished. We were lucky enough to survive this tragedy, but that comes with a heavy burden of responsibility to not be silent.

Although these stories are only a small fraction of the voices and experiences that deserve to be heard, they bring to life the true spirit of the human condition and our collective drive to survive, to protect, and to support. These are the incredible souls who form the community that I am proud to be a part of here in Lebanon; people who were here in the midst of the catastrophe, and many who are still here, continuing, against all odds, to mobilize, organize, and strive for truth and justice, to build a better country. Because a better Lebanon can be realized. Let's build it.

—Zeina Saab, April 2023

One hundred percent of the royalties from book sales will be donated to support victims of the Beirut explosion.

Thank you for your support.

To learn more, please visit www.bsgbeirut.com.

NOTE FROM THE EDITOR

"Ethics is about how we inhabit uncertainty, together."—Brian Massumi

Both Rawi Hage's foreword and Zeina Saab's introduction work through the significance of this collection of accounts of the Beirut port explosion as an incessant demand for accountability; that is, not simply for the atrocities of August 4, but of an ongoing collapse of which the blast is but one terribly violent symptom. Continuing to remember and share our respective experiences in a context that allows such tragedy to happen is a gesture of—dare I say—hope. Not a dreamy kind of hope, but a disciplined one, bold and rebellious in the simple act of defiance of waking up in the morning and confronting another day of unpredictability.

To me, the importance of *Beyond Shattered Glass* was—and continues to be—in its process of becoming. Writing is a collective act, and this book is a testament to the significance and possibility of writing together in a way that recognizes and acknowledges the complexities of our individual and shared experiences.

In addition to the named authors and contributors who worked hard to tell the stories printed on these pages, many voices—loud and silent, through support or critique—have given shape to these texts and made this book possible. Of course, these accounts don't tell everyone's story (we could never), but they do offer various encounters with a diverse, often challenging and conflictual, social fabric that is Lebanon. And so these stories are a sign of defiant hope, of the power of writing together in an attempt to make sense of all the unknown and find meaning through the uncertainty, one single sentence at a time.

—RL Attieh, April 2023

I. ON SURVIVAL

She's Not OK

S amar was clutching her hand, turning her wedding ring round, and round, a nervous habit she had picked up when she was first married, all those lifetimes ago. Only a few minutes earlier she had turned to Salim and told him not to worry, that the lines were jammed because so many people were trying to reach loved ones, and doesn't he remember the war? She assured him that Georgette's phone was just jammed and she'd be home any minute. After all, she was coming all the way from Hamra. There must be traffic, she said, and poured him another *finjein* of coffee. He worried so much; he always had.

Thirty-three years ago, when Georgette, the last of their three children, was born, they both agreed that they now understood what love at first sight was. How silly they were to think that this kind of love existed in anything other than the children they would have together. How naïve they were then, believing in things that gave them comfort simply because they wanted or needed to. How silly they were.

We have grown too old; we are no longer silly, Samar thought. A small whisper in the recesses of her subconscious brain began to form, but she couldn't quite make out what it was saying. *She's fine*, she thought. The small shards of glass around the living room floor glistened from the remaining light that snuck its way through the hollowed-out windows. Samar had cleaned up as much as she could, but she knew all too well that when glass shattered, you were bound to miss some. It was for this reason that she believed shattered glass remained forever. There was some from the bombings during the war, some from the kids playing in the house and breaking an ashtray she loved, or some glass figurine she couldn't seem to place. But this time, there was so much more. It shattered around them all at once. The windows, all the windows. That was when she knew that they would no longer stay in this apartment. No, they would have to move. *Too much shattered glass here. Definitely too much shattered glass. We'll never be able to find it all.*

She looked over at Salim. He was staring at the carpet and she wondered if he was thinking the same thing: *Shattered glass remains forever.*

They had only just learned that the explosion came from the port. Samar thought it was at their doorstep. Later she would find out that everyone thought that. Everyone in Beirut. Oh Beirut! She wondered about Gemmayze, about the beloved Ashrafieh neighborhood. About Beirut the city and Beirut the people.

"Good thing Georgette's work is so far from the port. She's fine." This time she said it out loud. Salim worried so much.

Georgette is fine, it's the traffic on the streets and in those intricate synapses of the phone lines. She gave her ring one more spin and then she heard it. The whisper. She stood up and looked around the living room as if seeing it for the first time. It was 7:22 PM. When Salim asked her where she was going, all she could say was, "She's not OK." She grabbed her purse.

It's a small pleasure really, but it's important to me, you know? The things that make you feel good help you make others feel good, don't they? I mean, like a smile, right? Sure, it's not everything, but I like to look pretty. No that's not it. I don't like to look pretty, I like to feel pretty. And this is something just for me. That's what I was telling Nathalie. Not many people understood what I meant, but she did. Once you find the person who knows how to do your nails, you'll go to the ends of the Earth for her. It's a big deal, I swear. She laughed when I said that. The little things, Nathalie, those are the mysterious freckles of happiness that make the world turn. She was glad that I was there that day, in the new salon where she worked. She was glad I had come all the way to Gemmayze, even though it's so out of my way, but I needed her.

"Isn't it strange that you can need strangers? I'm not going anywhere else," I assured her. "Where you go, I go." I stretched my hand out in front of me and admired the color of the fresh polish. I did feel pretty.

Assaad was the patriarch of Georgette's work family. He didn't think of himself that way, but everyone else did. Everyone—Amin, Saad, Nisrine, Hussein, Georgette, Maya, Bilal—they all thought so. The papa, the *khayy*, the uncle, 'Ammo Assaad, though they never called him that. He was too close to be called 'ammo. They all worked together in the administrative sections of the Children's Cancer Center, so they thought of themselves as better equipped for tragedy—harder than most, all in all, tough. You would have to be. Assaad of course knew better. Maybe it was his age, or maybe it was his vivid memory of the war that taught him tragedy was not to be taken for granted, no matter how often it occurred. Maybe it was because he was the work papa, but he knew that you could never truly be equipped for what happened that day. He knew this and yet, when he looked down at his hands, he was still surprised that they were shaking. *The first phase is shock*, he thought, and then he remembered what shock did to him. It helped him formulate a plan, it made him a man of action, a doer. No time to think, just move. *Move!*

He picked up his phone to text anyone and everyone he loved. And they were many. Assaad loved big and loved well and loved without calling it love.

"I'm OK, but how are you?" "How's your family?" "Is this little one crying?" "How's your mother?" "Did you drink water?" "Don't breathe in the air." "Stay away from the balconies." "Tell the children they are safe; they need to hear it." So many messages, all of them answered, as he made a mental checklist of his personal circle of immediate survivors. The work group chat was also checking in, and Assaad made a whole new sub-checklist. Colleagues, the kids, as he affectionately called them. Maya, Hussein, Bilal, Georgette. He stopped. *Georgette? Georgette. I didn't hear from her. I don't think I did.* He checked the text-chain, went all the way up to 6:07 PM. He flinched again, just like when he was pushed back by the pressure of the blast. *That's just the shock.* He adjusted the checklist and yes, so many texts, and they were still coming. His phone was still buzzing *hamdillah*. They say "We are safe," but nothing from Georgette. The group chat had started to repeat her name just as he was thinking, *Has anyone spoken to Georgette? She's not answering.* Assaad exhaled, only then realizing that he had been holding his breath. *The shock,* he thought, *there it is again.* It was 6:55 PM. Assaad grabbed his face mask and headed out the door.

They had a plan. They needed a plan. Because *what else can you do right now? A plan is something I can hang onto and a plan will keep me safe. A plan will keep Georgette safe. Mama and Baba are coming, baby girl, we have a plan, don't you worry.* Salim was the driver, parking would be a nightmare, and they had to move quickly. Samar didn't want to be in the front seat. *I'm the lookout on the left side, so I need to be in the back.* Her daughter-in-law was in the front seat, so she'd be the right-side lookout. Cover their bases. Her son was in another car so they could cover more ground. *Then we'll coordinate. Good thing there's internet, cell phones, not like the war. This is not like the war.* Then Samar had a thought that would persist in the months to come: *This is worse than the war.* She looked out her window, glancing along the highway and inner roads on her way to Gemmayze, to the port area where it happened. She heard Salim's voice on the phone calling an extended family member who worked at Roum Hospital.

"Is Georgette there?" she heard Salim say. "Is she at Roum Hospital? Will you check for us?" There was a pause on the line, and Samar heard the answer from the other end.

"It's gone, *khalo.* The hospital is gone." Even though the voice on the other end was faint, Samar could clearly hear it breaking from one word to the next.

Mama's coming, baby girl, your whole family is coming, don't you worry. And that's when she saw it, and she gasped. Forum de Beyrouth, in all its steel monstrosity, was reduced to what looked like a crumpled piece of paper.

Their car slowed and came to a full stop; in front of them were lines of charred vehicles, some parked, others in the middle of the road. These cars were driving along this road and they had people in them.

Tombs, Samar thought, *empty tombs, but where are the people now?* That's when she heard herself screaming, "My daughter is out there! Let me pass, let me pass!" The police officer was at their car window gesturing for them to turn around, and even though he was avoiding eye contact with Samar, he couldn't help but glance at her. His eyes betrayed a glint of pity—or maybe it was just the remaining moments of his youthful innocence. He quickly turned away from Samar and told Salim the roads to take to enter Ashrafieh from the back end, like he was sharing a secret. He stepped back a few paces and rubbed his eyes before returning to his post.

Assaad met his colleagues at their office in Hamra. There was debris, an eerie snowfall of charcoal dust, and everywhere, the subdued faces of people trudging past him. Later, he heard someone call them zombies and he wondered if he looked like that too. The wreckage consisted of glass, rubble, the leaves of trees bent out of shape, and the trash left in and around those ugly green containers without lids. The air was swimming with dust and paper particles and floating plastic bags and black residue and that haze of charcoal snow. The American University of Beirut Medical Center across the street had waves of taxis dropping off bloodied people who were being held up by those who could walk. Others were arriving in ambulances. Some were even on the backs of motos. Georgette wasn't there, that much they knew. Assaad wondered if she was somehow in transit, if some random stranger agreed to give her a ride on the back of his moto. *She's probably never been on one*, he thought, realizing that he was gaping at the sight of it all. He looked at his younger colleagues, and they were doing the same. He had to take charge. They had two motos between them, so the four of them would be on the search.

Information was seeping in about Georgette's whereabouts, in the form of buzzing notifications on WhatsApp chats. *She went to do her nails in CityMall?* Assaad wasn't convinced. *No. CityMall is too far from the epicenter to keep Georgette from answering her phone. She wouldn't do that. And it's close to her home. Georgette would have found her way.* He didn't say any of this out loud; he just needed to move. So they moved. The motos were winding through the traffic, around glass and building debris as they headed through Ashrafieh to get to the other side of town. Assaad felt blessed to be driving; he needed to focus on something other than what he saw in front of him. One thought did sneak its way in as the destruction surrounding him burned itself into his memory: *It's a miracle that anyone could have survived this.* He shook the thought away and kept winding past mangled cars and destroyed people.

Samar will never forget the sight of it. The sheer destruction. The buildings with gaping holes where walls used to be. A mattress caught up in electrical wire. *That was someone's bed.* Clothes and appliances scattered here and there, and the blood. The blood. The blood. On cars. On the street. On people. *On that woman's dress—it's soaked.* The car stopped; they had arrived at Rizk Hospital and Salim, God bless him, would take care of parking the car. Samar jumped out and headed towards the front entrance, where a huge crowd was fighting with the barricade of soldiers trying to maintain order. They pushed people back and back and farther back. A local journalist was clutching her microphone, her knuckles white as she tried to remain composed in front of the camera. There were five like her, each focused on their cameras so as not to break down in despair. "From the port…" "Loss of life is still unknown …" "Total chaos behind me …" "No answer, only blood." Samar grabbed her daughter-in-law and led her to the back area, where they found another crowd of people screaming to get in.

"I need to find my husband."

"Is my son in there?"

"What's the matter with you!"

"Let me in! Let me in!" Samar wasn't sure if she was screaming with them. A fight broke out between a man who was looking for his wife and a soldier who was stopping him.

Hand in hand, Samar snuck them both in past the commotion, and for a split second she was proud of her resourcefulness, until she saw the silent tears of a young boy smearing the blood on his cheeks. Her momentary relief was interrupted by the reality of the day. *Georgette.* The boy was being stitched up in the hospital's hallway. So was the woman with the gash on her arm. So was the man clutching a pack of cigarettes, his bloodied fingers staining the open box revealing filters splattered in the same red color that spread across the whole hospital. On walls. On the floor. On the blue scrubs of its staff who were running around with a force of concentration that could only be defined as heroism. The blood. The blood. The blood. A morbid modern art painting. *Georgette.* Samar's legs carried her from floor to floor, each the same scene of horror, just different players. *Georgette. I'll find you. I'm going to find you, baby girl.*

Roum was destroyed—no point in going there. Geitawi—half gone. Mar Yousef, Haroun Hospital, Hotel Dieu, Arz Hospital—they had been to all of them, and they were told the same thing over and over again.

"We have no time to take names. Search for yourselves." The nurses and doctors were overwhelmed and seemed numb. For every person sent to the ICU, ten more would show up. By the last hospital on their tour, Assaad felt the numbness creep into his body. He shivered. *She's not safe.*

"Rizk Hospital," he said. "We need to go there."

It was past 9 PM when Samar left Rizk to meet with Salim. Her daughter-in-law was holding her up as they walked past the news cameras. One of the reporters stopped them and Samar started repeating: "Her name is Georgette Aoude, she's missing, she's been missing. Georgette, Georgette Aoude." She didn't quite remember turning away from the cameras. Time started to skip and jump around her. Samar's head was heavy with fear. And then she heard her name: "*Tante Samar?*"

Assaad's moto pulled up to Rizk hospital. He surveyed the situation and tried to formulate the best way inside, bracing himself for another walk through the mayhem of injuries and death. He walked by the cameras and heard Georgette's name. At first he thought it was his imagination, but there it was again.

"Georgette," and then nothing. He turned around and saw her. "*Tante Samar?*"

Samar looked at him, confused. Then she looked past him and saw Bilal and recognized them all. For the first time since she heard the whisper in the back of her subconscious; Samar started sobbing. She could no longer hold herself up. She sat on the ground and let the tears flow through her fingers and onto the pavement.

Salim had arrived by then and was holding his wife. Assaad had made sure she had water and continued to rest. They sat with her on the ground and did the only thing they knew how to do—they went over the plan. They discussed what hospitals they had visited. Salim double-checked his phone for the messages from his son, who was scouting on his own. Twenty young men from Anfeh, their village, had just arrived in Beirut and were doing their own hospital rounds, in case they had missed her. They were taking shifts, and "they wouldn't rest before they got answers." That's what they said, the boys from Anfeh. It was clear now that there was an army of people searching for Georgette, and this gave Samar some comfort, even though she couldn't voice it at the moment. Instead, she just nodded as she took in all the names of the hospitals that didn't have Georgette and clutched her husband's hand as he patted her softly on the back. Someone told someone who told someone else that she was doing her nails in Gemmayze, not in CityMall.

"Is that confirmed?" It took Samar a moment to process this information, and she squinted her eyes to make sure she understood right. *Gemmayze. The eye of the storm. The center of it all.* Samar got up to leave.

They parked as close as they could to the salon where she was doing her nails. *Maybe she had left already,* Samar thought. *Maybe she had finished and left and then lost her phone and then got a small cut, so she's doing the right thing and going to the hospital. But I've seen the hospitals, so even with just a tiny little wound she's probably spending hours there and then, if I know my daughter, habibte Georgette, she's probably helping others because that's what she would do and that's why it's been so long and I still haven't found her. It's been so long since*—No. Salim and Samar walked silently through the streets of Gemmayze. Salim looked up for falling stones from the old buildings or down to the dangerous debris blocking their path, while Samar stared straight ahead until she came face-to-face with Georgette's parked car. Bent inward from its roof. *Demolished.*

Time was warped, bending almost, when Samar found herself at Mount Lebanon Hospital, as if she just woke up there suddenly. They had heard from someone, who told someone, who knew someone at the Red Cross, that Georgette was taken there. They were sure of it, and so there Samar was, going up and down stairs, through the hallways, entering every single room, sometimes twice. She was just going where her legs took her. "Try the COVID section, maybe they took her there," said a nurse passing by. Samar followed where the nurse had pointed and thought about the COVID patients. She looked at her husband and her daughter-in-law. They looked so tired and so, something she couldn't quite pinpoint. After an hour and a half, at almost 11:30 PM, Samar knew what she had seen on their faces. She imagined she looked like that too. She saw it in the eyes of the COVID patients, in the weariness of the injured waiting their turn to get stitched up. It was the loss of hope, and it was everywhere she looked.

Assaad's network had just heard that the Red Cross didn't take Georgette because she was walking and talking, a gash on her head, but not severe enough to take space in the ambulance. They had to prioritize. They had to leave so many people behind. On that day, making those decisions was part of their job, but they didn't know Georgette like Asaad did. She was so sensitive, in the words she used, the way she talked to people, how she was careful with everything she said or did. *There's no way she would be walking around if she was wounded.* There just wasn't.

Lebanon is like that, you know. It's one small town inside a country. Everyone knows each other somehow, and everyone needs each other at some point. It really does feel like one big family, extended out into branches that are built not only by blood but by goodwill. We always need each other. We have no one else, you see. We are each other's security blanket. That's how it happened that day. Before I lost it all to darkness, my eyes were open and blinking and I saw them, the two women who found me and carried me. They couldn't find a car and insisted that the old man driving his taxi deliver me to the nearest hospital. Then there was the best friend of the sister-in-law of a friend of mine who went to Arz Hospital to support her mother, a nurse, called in on a code blue, or is it a code red like the movies? She had social media and knew she needed to do something, so she took pictures of the injured at the ICU, and of the dead as well. And of the nameless, the lost. They were circulated on WhatsApp groups. I was lost and she found me, the girl with the pictures. She recognized me because of my manicured nails, and she found my family from the tree branches of our community. There they were, rushing around. And then there was me. Still. In total darkness. Floating away from myself.

When Samar saw Georgette, her head was wrapped up in large white bandages, polka-dotted with blood across her temple. Her eyes were covered up and tubes were coming out of her mouth, but it was her. It was Georgette. *What have they done to you, my sweet girl?* And that's when Samar blacked out in a mixture of relief and sheer exhaustion. A new fear crept up on her, unsure if her girl would wake up, or what she would be like if she ever did. *We'll make sure your nails are clean and proper, my sweet girl, so all the nurses, doctors and surgeons and us, all of us, will know, Georgette is still here.*

From that point forward, Samar had no more memories, only pictures of the days to come. Salim reading stories to Georgette after her first operation, holding her hand through the coma and pointing the video chat towards her so that her sister in the States could sing to her. Holding her hand again when her sister came on that long flight from the States just to stroke Georgette's forehead in person. She saw her son pacing the room and then silently weeping by Georgette's bedside. She saw her daughter-in-law bringing cups of coffee. She saw Georgette's work friends and her manager visit with food and comforting words. She saw nurses laughing wholeheartedly at the sheer positivity that surrounded her daughter. She saw herself smiling for the first time in a long time when they removed a layer of bandages and she saw Georgette's face again. She looked like an angel. *Of course you would think so, Mom. That's what Georgette would have said,* Samar laughed to herself. And prayer. So much prayer. Samar must have memorized the texture and cracks of that hospital room ceiling, and later she would marvel that her rosary beads did not completely disintegrate under the weight of her faithful fingers. *The whole world is praying for you, my darling. Wake up, my sweet girl. Please wake up.* Samar turned her wedding ring round and round, then she stopped and took Salim's hand and squeezed.

I was doing my nails, and the next thing I know, I woke up one month later in the hospital. My mom was next to me, she's the first person that told me. All she said was, "Don't worry, don't worry, you're fine, you were in this accident and you're fine now." A couple of words, a bit confusing, sure, but I don't remember a thing. I didn't hear anything. I didn't see anything. I don't feel pain and I have no trauma. I only saw my pretty nails, and then I woke up again in the hospital. They said that my pretty nails helped me get recognized, isn't that funny? When I looked down that day when I woke up, my nails were still so clean and well kept. My family made sure of that. My poor family. My poor parents, my friends from work. They went through a lot. Each day for weeks after that, they would visit me with gifts. There was a day of cakes, another of balloons and flowers. One time a whole *rakweh* of coffee, my favorite perfume, scented candles, lunches. There will forever be a gap in my memory while I was sleeping in that coma, but it's filled with an image I will never forget: the whole team, more than thirty of them, dressed in white and holding red balloons. They stood outside, and I looked down from my hospital room window. I had only just learned to walk and talk again and there they were, with a sign that said, "WE LOVE YOU." They cheered and cheered and cheered through a megaphone, and they gave me the biggest gift of all. For the first time ever, I realized how many people truly care about me. For the first time it became clear, you know? I am loved. And I'm still here. I am alive and I am loved. I am loved. I am here.

Written by Nadia Tabbara
Story contributed by Georgette Aoude and Samar Aoude

Afterword

Georgette was one of the many people who were severely injured that day, and luckily she survived. This story is from the perspective of her mother and one of her colleagues as they frantically searched for Georgette, but the reality of the day was that countless people worked to find her and to support the family during this harrowing ordeal. George, her brother, was in the second car, driving around in the mayhem while his wife Carine, her beloved sister-in-law, was tireless in her efforts searching hospitals and social media. Zeina, Georgette's sister, traveled from the States, leaving her family behind to spend a month in the hospital next to her. Hana, the general manager of The Children's Cancer Center where Georgette works, was constantly connecting doctors and medical administrators with the family in an effort to find her in the many hospitals that were completely overwhelmed that fateful night. In the days and the months that followed, all of these people and many more friends, colleagues, even strangers who knew Georgette's story were instrumental in her recovery and her positive outlook on life. They are too many to name, but they live inside this story, between the lines and in the white space of emotion that cannot be filled with words.

Her Name Is Eleni

The Ethiopian Airlines plane revved up its engines into a roar as it left Bole International Airport and soared over the sprawling city of Addis Ababa. Within its belly, more than two hundred Ethiopian citizens clutched nervous hands over the ends of their arm rests. There were no tourists among them, no diplomats, no children, and no elders. Only young, strong people, mostly women, heading to Beirut for labor and domestic work. Those who sat by the windows looked outside as their capital city of five million grew smaller. Five million mothers and fathers, husbands and wives, sons and daughters, friends and lovers. It was for those people that everyone on the plane was leaving. Most would not be back for two years, some for even longer.

It is for her mother that Eleni was going to Beirut for the second time. To earn a living as a domestic worker in a stranger's house. An old lady living alone. Her salary will be many times more than she could ever earn in her homeland. It will help with her mother's medical bills. They might save a little even. It's not how she dreamed she would be spending her youth. It's not where anyone on the plane dreamt of going when they traveled. But it is where everyone was going today.

Eleni was startled when the passenger next to her reached across her seat and unlocked her beverage tray. The flight attendant pushing the thin metal cart had reached their row. The passenger smiled knowingly at Eleni, as if she was hearing her thoughts this whole time. "You will be OK," the passenger said kindly. Eleni smiled back and realized that tears were rolling down her face. She wiped them quickly with the back of her sleeve and nodded repeatedly: "Yes. Yes. God willing we will. All will be OK!"

Three days after the explosion, volunteers were spilling into the hard-hit area of Mar Mikhael. Karim was one of the young people arriving to help however they could. He stopped in middle of the road, or what used to be a road, and leaned on his broom under the searing August sun. He wanted to take a deep breath, but decided against it. His face mask might have been helpful during the pandemic, but it was absolutely useless against the acrid chemical smell that filled the air. He stared in awe at the level of destruction surrounding him. Karim was used to challenges. He was a rising star in a large global corporation. He was an activist for human rights of migrant workers in Lebanon. He was familiar with the kind of hard work required to bring about change. *But how could this mess be fixed with a broom,* he asked himself, as he wiped the beads of sweat collecting on his brow. *How?*

To his left, a destroyed entrance of an old building beckoned. He started walking towards it, carefully negotiating the broken concrete and mangled steel between them. He arrived at an opening where the building door frame used to be. Maybe he was called in by the shade, or by some sounds he heard from the floors above. He wasn't sure why, but he started climbing up the stairs, unaware of the invisible hands of fate guiding his way. There was fresh blood on the walls. Many times the smell made him want to turn around and run back out, but he didn't. Two floors up, he reached an apartment with a missing front door and peaked inside. There were volunteers cleaning up a living room. One side of the room featured a balcony fully denuded of its French doors, revealing an unobstructed view of the Beirut port. Lines of red smoke were still meandering up from its broken silos, adding dramatic color to a large blue sky over a shimmering calm sea. A warm Mediterranean breeze pulled him back inside. An old lady was curled up on a couch in the middle of the room. He took a few steps and kneeled beside her. They started to talk.

Her name was Therese. She lived alone. She was here when the explosion happened. And now she lived in a house with no windows and no doors. He asked if he could get her anything.

"A Diet Coke," she replied. He could have used a Diet Coke himself. He retraced his steps down the bloody staircase again. No shop survived, but thirty minutes later he returned with some cold cans and snacks for everyone. Therese and Karim popped open the cans and started chatting, when Therese suddenly asked, "Where is Eleni? I haven't seen her since the blast."

"Who is Eleni?" Karim responded, surprised. The blast was days ago.

"She's my Ethiopian helper," Therese said after taking another sip of her cold soda. "She was making dinner in the kitchen when it happened."

After some nudging, Therese got up from her couch and went into her bedroom. She retrieved Eleni's passport from a safe. Karim stared at the picture of the young Black woman on the first page. She had a large forehead, made more prominent because her hair was pulled back from her face. She was born in January in Addis Ababa. Karim made the calculation in his head. She should be thirty-two years old now. She looked much younger in her passport photo. Karim took a snapshot of the front page with his phone. He cropped her picture and posted it on social media sites like Locate Victims Beirut, asking if anyone had seen her. To find a victim in the chaos of post-blast Beirut was not easy. There were thousands of pictures of missing people on these sites, hundreds of them of Ethiopian domestic workers. The healthcare system in Beirut was in disarray after the destruction of three hospitals, and it was unlikely Therese would hear about Eleni anytime soon.

Unsure of what to do next, he left Therese and the seaside view and returned to the blood-stained stairs, unaware that some of the blood was Eleni's. He thought of that young woman utterly alone, distraught in some hospital ward, with no one by her side. His heart reached out for all the non-Lebanese victims, far from home without a family to lean on in what was probably the most terrifying time of their lives. As he approached the ground floor, a determination was slowly brewing inside of him. By the time he was exiting the building Karim had decided: Eleni wouldn't be alone anymore. He would find her.

The young nurse dropped the used needle into the sharps box after changing the intravenous line. When he took his latex gloves off, they made a loud pop, but he was not worried about waking his patient. She had been in a coma for more than a week.

He stared briefly at the young Ethiopian woman lying still in the ICU bed. Deep purple bruises were set around her nose and under her eyes, accentuating a severely swollen face. Layers of white gauze were wrapped tightly around her thick black hair. A clear plastic tube was pushed down her windpipe, connecting her lungs to the ventilator that helped her breathe.

The nurse walked around the bed and picked up her chart. On top of the page, the patient was identified as "Unknown Ethiopian Citizen." Various injuries were listed. Head and organ trauma. Broken bones. Patient 805, as she was known around the ICU, had been in a coma since she was brought in on August 4. She was on life support, but her vital signs were stable. There was no telling what would happen next. The nurse made some notes and placed the chart back. It saddened him that no one came asking about her, that no one knew her name.

"Who are you, Patient 805?" the nurse asked the air in the room.

Only the blinking machines answered back, and the answer was always the same: "Beep … Beep … Beep …"

To Karim, everything that mattered before the explosion felt secondary: his work, his summer vacation plans, the demonstrations of downtown Beirut. Now his days were dominated by frontline demands: reconnecting the hard-hit areas with a data network through his job, volunteering in Mar Mikhael, and looking for Eleni. He posted her picture on every site for the missing, to no avail. Then he started calling upon friends and family who worked in hospitals in the area, sending them her passport picture, asking them to ask around. Finally, a cousin who worked at the AUB Medical Center told him about a coma patient in the ICU she had heard about.

"Maybe it's her," his cousin said. "Bring us her passport."

The next day, Karim was at the hospital with the passport he got from Therese. He met his cousin, as well as a doctor, a nurse and a social worker. They stood outside a glass wall, staring at an unconscious intubated woman in the intensive care ward. She was a stranger to them, and they were strangers to each other. The nurse walked in with the picture and examined Patient 805's face intently. He walked out and nodded.

"I believe it's her," he said. "I believe patient 805 is Eleni."

They all smiled a muted smile. Karim would have liked to have found her in better conditions, but at least they knew where she was.

An employee entered her name in a computer. From then on, everyone in the hospital knew who she was. When they discussed her case, they called her by her name.

"How is Eleni today?" they would ask. The embassy was finally able to notify her family.

"Eleni is alive," they reported. Church friends were able to find her and came to visit at the hospital.

"Dear God, save your Eleni and bring her back to us again," they prayed.

I am not OK, Eleni thought. *I am not OK.*

She lay on a hospital bed in a darkness pierced only by the blue and red blinking lights of many machines around her. She was connected to the machines by strings of wires, some glued to her chest, some wrapped around her arm, and some clutched around her fingers. Fluid streamed into her veins from plastic bags hanging to the left of her head. Sometimes she felt the cold liquid travel up her arm and through her shoulder and into her neck, sending goose bumps down her spine. Mostly the machines were quiet, but every once in a while, they decided to ping and beep, maybe to check if she's still there. She waited for the sound as she stared at the ceiling. The waiting distracted her from the pain returning to her head and her leg. Soon she would have to press the button to get the night nurse to administer more pain medication that would lull her into an uncomfortable sleep.

She didn't want to sleep again. Not yet. She had slept for too long. For a whole month, they told her. "A coma," they called it. A terrifying place between life and death, where not even God's angels dared to go. After the Beirut blast, everyone experienced four long weeks. But for Eleni, it was a blink of an eye. One minute she was sitting on a small stool in her employer's kitchen before preparing dinner, the next minute she was waking up terrified in a hospital bed. Her eyelids closed to one reality and opened up to a whole new one. Four weeks packed into the blink of an eye.

Her fingers reached for the button placed by her hand on the bed. The night nurse appeared by her side and smiled reassuringly as she gently patted her arm.

"Are you OK Eleni? Do you want more pain medication?" the nurse asked in Arabic.

"Yes please," she said, but thought, *No, I am not OK.*

She was there again in that familiar place, suspended between the ceiling and the floor. Her phone flew out of her hand with a text to her mother that was never sent. She could feel a force, a wind, blowing on her cheeks. She could see the wooden balcony door flying towards her and an unearthly orange glow from beyond above the sea. In all the times she relived it, she never heard the explosion. She never even had the time to be afraid. She knew what happened next. The old refrigerator would fly up and hit her from behind. Then they would both fall, and she would land beneath it on the floor. But this time, from inside the old fridge above her, she heard an unfamiliar sound. A giggle. Someone was giggling inside the fridge. She looks up but her eyes are closed. *Open your eyes Eleni*, she tells herself. *Open your eyes.*

A handsome young man stood by her bed, and turned towards her when she stirred. He wore a face mask, but she could see his smile through his eyes. He had prematurely salt-and-pepper hair, despite his youthful appearance. Her Ethiopian visitors, women she knew from church who checked on her often, were sitting on chairs set around her hospital bed.

"Eleni, Karim is here," one of the women said, and giggled again, as if his name demanded it.

"Karim is back to see you," said another.

"Hi Karim," she said, struggling to speak against the pull of sedatives and her sore throat.

"How are you, Eleni?" he said kindly.

"OK," she lied.

"*Yalla*," Karim asserted. "Get better soon so you can go home. I can imagine how much your mother wants to see you." To that, the ladies nodded vigorously in unison.

Eleni smiled at everyone again, but not for long. The pain and medication were ever present, weighing down her consciousness. Her smile faded promptly as she closed her eyes and drifted away.

The women around her continued their chatter as Karim said goodbye and left the hospital room. He sighed deeply as he walked down the sterile white hallways to the exit. Eleni waking up after a month in coma was the miracle he needed to feel hopeful again, to feel that they could all recover. He could see that she didn't feel as hopeful yet. He made a wish for her as he ventured out from the hospital's glass atrium to the billowing streets of Beirut. The humid September air rapidly congealed into a layer of moisture on his cool skin. Karim turned left on a street and disappeared into the river of humanity rushing through the city's one-way lanes.

Eleni was suspended again between the floor and the ceiling. Her phone was moving away from her hand and the balcony doors towards her. The fridge was ready to pounce, and the fiendish red ball was expanding like a mushroom above the sea, but instead of that forceful familiar wind she now felt a warmth on her cheeks that was like sunshine.

Open your eyes Eleni, she insisted. *Open your eyes.*

She tried, but it was too bright. The uncomfortable sofa she was sleeping on was positioned just under a window in a living room where the summer sun flooded in through white lace curtains. She was unsure if it was morning or afternoon. She could see that two young girls were sharing an armchair across the small room. A coffee table filled the space between them. Above her, resting on the back of the sofa and under the window, were three red teddy bears and a colorful poster of the Virgin Mary carrying baby Jesus. The air smelled of Ethiopian coffee, as if it was made in that space hundreds of times. She struggled to remember where she was until it gradually came to her as she sat up.

When Eleni was told she had to leave the hospital bed that had been her home for almost eight weeks, she was far from relieved. She still couldn't walk on her own, her vision was blurred, and her speech slurred. There was also the bigger problem of where she would go. She couldn't board a plane because her injuries put her at high risk of complications. Her employer, Therese, would not take her back into the destroyed apartment. Then Sami, an Ethiopian man who worked for an NGO that helped migrant workers, found Salam, an Ethiopian woman who had been living in Lebanon for a long time. Salam volunteered to shelter Eleni until she was well enough to travel. She lived in a one-bedroom apartment with her two young daughters.

The apartment was in a building without an elevator in the southern suburb of Ouzai. The streets were narrow and crowded, and so was the apartment. The couch in the living room was all she had to offer Eleni during her recovery. The couch was small and stiff, but it was still an overwhelming kindness by a stranger who had so little to give, yet gave what she had. Eleni was grateful. Salam helped her with her medication, and Sami arranged for a driver to pick her up weekly for physical therapy at a nearby medical center. She had to be carried up and down the stairs.

Karim was also there for her. He became the contact between her, the NGO that Sami worked for, and the medical staff at the AUB Medical Center. He coordinated her paperwork and went back to her employer to get what was needed. After helping Therese for many years, she now needed help just to get through the day. In a country where she had no family and knew almost no one, she was grateful that so many were coming to her aid.

The recovery work was painful and slow. Her legs sustained multiple injuries, and she could only walk with the aid of a metal cane they gave her. The physiotherapists encouraged her to make little movements and gave her exercises to do at home. She wasn't sure any of it was helping. Her days were also dotted with bouts of dizziness and nausea. Other than the appointments, she went nowhere and had few visitors. Salam was very welcoming, but the pandemic restricted everyone's movements. The young girls, upon discovering that Eleni rarely talked and never played, left her to her thoughts and dreams. In the hours she was lucid, she wondered if she'd ever walk again, work again, get married and have children.

What will become of me and my mother when I return to Addis Ababa? How will we survive?

She came to Beirut for a better future, to help her mother and save some money. She had lost everything and was much worse off now than before she left her own country. She had nothing left but her disabilities. When she tried to think of her future, all the doors closed, and the air became heavy. And from that air there was no escape. The window above her couch announced the beginning and end of days, as they rolled and rolled in a blur.

Eleni was suspended between the floor and the ceiling. The doors were flying towards her and the phone has left her hand, but now she was holding rosary beads in its place. She was looking at the strange item, bewildered as she waited for the impact of the fridge on her back. But instead she is shaking. Someone is shaking her. A voice from the outside is calling her: "Wake up Eleni, wake up. Karim is here."

Karim had arranged for doctor appointments and said he would pick her up in the morning, but she wasn't sure he would come. Her doubt disappeared when Karim not only showed up but even carried her down the stairs. She was so embarrassed by the attention that she smiled through her nausea and pain. At the new private clinics building next to the hospital, they waited in one reception room after another to see a neurologist, an internist, an orthopedic surgeon, and an ophthalmologist. Eleni's medications were adjusted. She needed a new brace for her leg and new prescription glasses. It took twelve hours to get through all the appointments and paperwork. By the end of the day, they were both exhausted to the bone. Karim dropped her off and returned home to prepare a presentation for work. Life went on as normal outside Beirut, and he had to keep up with the two worlds vying for his attention.

Eleni was worn out but, for the first time, also strangely hopeful. The doctors insisted she'd get better. They probably sensed her despair; she was struggling with her slow progress after two months of therapy. Then there was Karim, waiting with her through every appointment, filling out all the paperwork, bringing her cold juice to soothe her throat, getting her the new medicine. She doubted any of her fellow migrant workers would've been able to make it through that medical administration maze. If so many people were doing so much for her, then maybe she should try harder not to disappoint them. If only she felt slightly better. If only she could imagine a better future.

With the new medications the nausea slowly subsided, and she was able to keep down food. It made a huge difference. Karim came to pick her up again. This time Salam and her two daughters joined them. He took them to the optician, where she chose oval gold frames for her new prescription glasses. They were ready in an hour and she gasped when she saw Karim and Salam in focus for the first time. *This is how the world looks?* She had almost forgotten.

Then they walked into a medical supplies store to pick up equipment for Eleni that the doctors prescribed. Karim told the store owner Eleni's story, how she almost died in the explosion, woke up from a coma, and was now recovering. Hearing her story, the owner stopped and stared at her awkwardly for a minute. She wasn't sure what was going on. He then bowed to her, straightened up, looked her in the eye, and spoke to her in a very serious manner. She couldn't understand him.

"What is he saying?" she asked Salam, who looked slightly stunned.

"He is apologizing," Salam said, incredulously. "He is apologizing for what has befallen you in his country. He's giving you the equipment for free, and he's apologizing!"

Eleni, Salam, and the girls were mesmerized, too confused to react. They had never seen this side of the Lebanese people. Eleni thanked the man in her hoarse voice and broken Arabic. It was beyond kindness. It was a moment of rare respect, and it made her feel bigger, stronger, physically better.

They walked over to a nice café at the Gefinor Center, a complex of white buildings full of offices. The autumn sun was gentle and warm, glistening against the white marble that tiled the large courtyard area. Eleni took a deep, liberating breath as she limped towards the café using her cane and Salam for support. They sat down and ordered lunch. The girls were over the moon when they were told they could get any of the fancy colorful cakes in the display case. Salam was in high spirits and chatting with Karim in Arabic. Eleni was quiet. The little Arabic she knew would not serve her well in casual conversation. Besides, her voice was still barely audible.

She admired the details now visible through her new glasses, and tried to take it all in. She was being waited on at a fancy café and had just received an apology from a man who had bowed to her. A familiar feeling was emerging that had long been forgotten. Hope. A small window opened onto another expansive white space. The world might be worth fighting for again. She promised herself to savor this moment.

Eleni was suspended between the floor and the ceiling. The big red cloud bloomed on the horizon. The balcony doors had left their frames and were rushing towards her. In one hand she felt the rosary beads, and then, without thinking, she raised the other hand quickly to shield her face. The unscripted move startled her awake and made her sit up on the couch and gasp.

Salam was sitting on the armchair across the room with a tray in her lap.

She looked up at Eleni.

"What's the matter, dear, did you have a nightmare?" She was peeling onions.

Eleni was on her feet now. She walked over to the sink to wash her face, leaving the walking cane behind the couch. All the little moves they made her do at physical therapy, again and again, had grown from tiny steps into bigger ones.

"Are we out of soap?" she yelled from the bathroom.

Her voice finally recovered, although it had gained a permanent rasp that she liked. *We have to get more soap before Karim arrives,* she thought. They had invited him for a final meal. The doctors had finally given her the OK to board a plane, and so she was returning to Addis. Wonderful Karim was bringing the paperwork to present to the airlines tonight. And he said he had a surprise!

She was so happy to finally be going home, with a changed face now hers again, a limp and an interesting new voice. And there remained the unknown omnipresent question: What now? What will I do? How will I live? But there was no time to go there. There was a traditional Ethiopian meal to cook, meat to be stewed, injera to bake, and soap to be bought. So much to be done before he arrived.

Later in the evening, Karim took a deep breath of the crisp winter air as he looked for his car in the dark, narrow lanes. The power was out in this part of Ouzai, but that did not dampen his mood. It felt so good to surprise Eleni with the good news. The woman who organized the social media group to locate Beirut victims was so inspired by their story that she started a fundraiser on a global platform. They raised more than $5,000 for Eleni, a life-changing amount of money! Eleni was elated, and so was everyone around her who had supported her through her recovery. Karim arranged for the funds to be transferred to her account in Addis. It was a global financial challenge to transfer money from a fundraising app in the UK to a bank in Ethiopia, but he found a way.

Four months ago, Karim stood helpless on the street of Mar Mikhael, wondering how a single person could make a difference in the face of such destruction. He felt desperate then, broken. Tonight he stood in the middle of another street with a heart full of joy. He was still broken, but now he was broken open. By watching Eleni get better, step by step and day by day, Karim snatched hope from the depths of incredible adversity. *We face helplessness by helping each other,* he thought, as he got into his car and closed the door.

They must've taken a hundred pictures that night. Eleni flicked her finger through each one, while her other hand busied itself with the rosary beads, studying the pictures carefully as the Ethiopian Airlines plane taxied to the tarmac at Beirut International Airport. They were all so happy in the tiny apartment in that over-crowded suburb of Beirut. The meat stew was great, but the injera was burned. They laughed at the injera. The joy in each picture made her laugh. The passenger next to her was amused.

"You got a lot friends in Beirut?" she asked. "How long did you stay?"

"Two years working, four months in recovering from the blast"

The passenger was perplexed. She looked at Eleni intently for a while and then there was a spark of recognition.

"You are the one! You are the one on TV! The one who woke up from a coma!"

Eleni smiled. The media was quite interested in her survival. There were blog posts and TV interviews and newspaper articles. She thought it might have been because of Karim. It was so unusual for a young Lebanese man to help an Ethiopian domestic worker as much as he did that local and social media deemed it worth documenting. She didn't mind. She loved Karim. He was her angel. Many people had saved her life in Beirut, but he found her among the lost and helped her return to her name. And that fundraising surprise! It gave her such a boost. She had come back from Beirut with more money than she ever dreamed of. For so long, the question on her mind was: *What will happen to me now?* The money transformed that question into much happier ones: *Should I start my own business? Should I buy a house?*

Money wasn't the only thing that dragged her out of her despair once she woke up from her long death-sleep. It was the social worker at the hospital, Sami working with the NGOs to pay her medical bills and release her from her employment contract, the countless women from church who visited her, brushed her hair, and prayed for her when she was in a coma, the social media campaign that located her after the explosion and raised money for her, Salam and her daughters and their tiny home, Karim and his big heart, the store owner

26

who bowed to her. The same city that tried to break her with a flying fridge and balcony door came together, person by person, stranger by kind stranger, group by group, to put her back together again.

The plane finally roars across the runway and levitates over Beirut. Eleni looks down at the jungle of concrete wedged between the Mediterranean and the majestic green mountains that rise from the sea. To the south, the sprawling coastal suburbs where Salam and the girls lived. On the opposite side of the city is the huge AUB Medical Center building where she spent months recovering, and farther to the north she can clearly make out the silhouette of the broken port silos. As the plane rises, the distance shrinks between these places, and she sees it all for the last time before leaving it all behind.

She has no idea what will come next, but as she clutches the ends of her armrests and closes her eyes, she knows this: She will be OK.

Written by Samira Kaissi
Story contributed by Eleni Wari and Karim Kattouf

The Wait for Deliverance

Note: Pseudonyms have been used throughout this story.

From Aleppo to Latakia

The roads were not new to Sabr, as he had often traveled between the two fashionable cities trading clothes. But this journey felt new. This time, he was escaping the bombing of Aleppo with his wife, their two children, and whatever belongings they could carry.

When the demonstrations across Syria turned violent, nobody in Aleppo expected the artillery, or that Aleppo would become a regional headquarters for the revolutionary army. Bombs rained on the city in the dead of night. Sabr witnessed his cousin's four-year-old become mute from trauma. He vowed that his children would not hear the sound of a bullet. Another cousin drove them to the government-controlled coast of Latakia. They were interrogated at several checkpoints—army, revolutionary and Islamist. Sabr used the same answers at each. Syrian checkpoints, where people are arrested for as little as removing stickers of the president from their cars, are notoriously unforgiving.

Sabr rented a small apartment in Latakia's poor neighborhood, Ramel al-Janubi, and began to look for work. His last business deal had left him ruined. He had not told his wife. She was under the impression he had found work selling clothes again. He had invested most of his bank capital in a clothing collection that was due to arrive in Latakia. But the shipping company casually informed him that the shipment was seized by terrorists, and they demanded ransom money. He owed the bank for the loan on his apartment, and could not pay off the hijackers. A cloud of suspicion haunted Sabr.

Who were the hijackers? Who was fighting whom? He couldn't say.

Sabr loved his young wife, Yasmeen, and their two sons more than any love he had known. He and Yasmeen grew up as distant cousins, and were barely newlyweds when the shocks began. Their eldest, Ali, was born with the first demonstrations, and their second, Mahmoud, with the first strikes on Aleppo. More than 20,000 Syrians died in the year between. Yasmeen was now in a new town, a new mother living far from her family for the first time. She went from living decently to barely being able to afford furniture.

Sabr had to save what he could. Yasmeen's few pieces of jewelry and the few thousand Syrian lira he had were their only nest egg. He combed the streets of Latakia's port area in search of work. One day, while he carried Ali, he met a familiar face from Aleppo. He knew that Abu Ibrahim worked in construction, and Sabr hastily offered his services as a day laborer. Abu Ibrahim quickly agreed and called him to work the next day. Sabr was shown a pile of three hundred concrete bricks, each weighing thirty-five pounds, and was tasked with carrying them up ninety steps. Sabr lifted the bricks onto his shoulders for relief, but usually he carried them with his hands, behind him on his lower back, so that he could stack two or three bricks up against his spine. This was his daily assignment for months.

Despite the heat of the summer and the humidity of the coast, Sabr only wore long-sleeve shirts, even to bed. He forbade his wife from entering the bathroom with him, especially when he showered. He swam in his clothes. Sabr would escape to the sea whenever he had the opportunity. He grew up by the sea, and taught himself to swim at a young age. Sabr felt the sea knew his secrets, and could answer him spiritually, no matter the question.

One day while at the beach with his family, one of Sabr's older brothers called with bad news. He tried to reassure Sabr.

"You're a faithful man. You've always been grateful to God, whatever happens. You said that your wife and kids are the most important thing, and you were able to escape. Anything material can be compensated. Money can be returned. Money is not everything."

Sabr thought his apartment must have been robbed, but his brother said heavily that the building was completely destroyed. The news fell on him like that pile of three hundred bricks. His enraged body tore through the water, the saltwater camouflaging his bitter tears. He thought about his life, his work, his lost savings, his family on the shore. Still in the water, Sabr thanked God and said to himself, "he who builds one house, can build another."

The newspapers called them indiscriminate airstrikes. Those who escaped death were abducted, tortured, or forced to take sides. Sabr struggled with his feelings that night. He cursed the war that did not know young from old, terrorist from freedom fighter. He cursed the war that destroyed everything in its path. Everyone had prayed to avoid another Lebanon. His wife's parents, too, were terrified for their lives and asked to join them in Latakia. His work, his home, everything was lost. It was finally time to tell his wife the truth.

Yasmeen sensed her husband's distress. After serving their evening tea, she looked at his hands and asked why they were scratched like that. Sabr was ready to confess everything. He explained to Yasmeen that it would be better for him to find work in Lebanon. It was impossible for anyone not from Latakia to find work or open a shop there. Prices had tripled, and rents were rising. Her brother already worked in Beirut, so Sabr called him for help. He rented another small apartment for his wife's family in the same building as theirs, packed what remained of his savings (approximately $5,000), and handed Yasmeen $1,000 so that she could afford her needs. Relieved that his wife and children were not alone, Sabr said to his wife, "I'm journeying into the unknown, to meet whatever God has written for us in this journey."

From Latakia to Beirut

The roads were not new to Sabr, as he had often traveled between the two fashionable cities trading clothes. But this journey felt new. He was now desperate for any work that could support his family until the Syrian war ended.

He wondered when he would see his wife and children again, this being the first time he had to leave them for more than a few days. He felt the war tightening around his body. When he reached Beirut, the independence and freedom of movement he felt was striking, in contrast to what he had just left. But Sabr knew immediately what would keep him there: "The fear of being unable to afford a piece of bread for my children! And the war is stretching," he answered his wife's brother, feeling strangled.

It was February 2013. Yasmeen's brother had arranged a meeting with his employer, Mr. Edward, who worked as a foreman for Mr. Malek, an engineer who owned several buildings. Sabr was assigned to carry bricks between buildings again, but he did it all with optimism. Mr. Edward recognized Sabr's eagerness and, when interviewing him, found a cultured tradesman who was forced into labor by war. Sabr was born and raised in Libya, living there until the age of twenty-seven; he had started working at age seven. The middle of seven sons, he built himself up to open his own restaurant, right next to his father's successful chain.

Mr. Edward instructed Sabr to do the delicate work of rewiring electrical faults and fixing water failures, and was soon praising him as talented and honorable. One morning, a fancy vehicle pulled into the site. Sabr didn't rush to it like his co-workers. The owner noticed, and walked over to ask his name. Sabr responded without redirecting his eyes from his work, as that was the dedication to safety expected on a construction site.

"May God bless you," the owner said kindly, and left.

Everyone that Mr. Malek asked had warm praise for Sabr, especially Mr. Edward, who said, "This human is a treasure that we must care for. He is knowledgeable and dedicated to work." Mr. Malek was convinced and instructed Mr. Edward to compensate Sabr's labor in cash. Sabr felt content. He was spared physical labor, and his employers were rewarding. He was energetic, but when he retired to his shared pension, he would recede into his lonely armchair to read a book or submit himself to memories of his wife and children. His tears carved into his thin face.

After two months of working six days a week, Sabr's longing reached a fever pitch. Sabr requested a holiday. Mr. Edward granted him two weeks. He rejoiced. The minutes leading up to his travel exhausted him. He bought gifts from the market, collected his savings, and set off on his return to Syria feeling overwhelmed.

The Return

The roads were not new to Sabr, as he had often traveled between the two fashionable cities trading clothes. But this journey felt new. There were army checkpoints everywhere, and Sabr's patience stretched thin. Every few kilometers passed like a doldrum.

He arrived in Latakia around two in the afternoon, his two kids in the street awaiting his arrival. Yasmeen was on the balcony, wearing all her accessories. Forgetting his luggage in the taxi, Sabr carried his children up the stairs, and together they hugged his wife. All his favorite meals were spread out on the table. He took his family shopping and to the beach promenade. As they passed the building Sabr had worked on, he said to Yasmeen, "I helped build this on my shoulders. I'm not ashamed to say I am a laborer." She praised God and her husband. Days passed like one long afternoon. On the last evening, Sabr kept the children up past their bedtime and woke them at dawn for one last embrace.

He returned to Beirut renewed. Love flowed from his eyes to the city that saved him. Sabr continued his pattern of work and holidays. Every two months, he felt the roads to Latakia bend time in a sluggish crawl, and return him in a flash. Their third child, Ayham, was born soon after, and, with this precious new bundle, Sabr's financial situation continued to stabilize.

No Address

Daesh entered the war in Syria in the summer of 2014 and crossed into Lebanon through illegal routes along the northern and Bekaa borders. The Lebanese government passed a new law that restricted all Syrians from entering Lebanon unless sponsored by a company or national. Sabr asked everyone he could for a *kafala*. Mr. Malek had already reached his quota for foreign visas, and all of his friends were in the same regrettable situation. By the time a friend introduced him to a willing sponsor, he was already at risk of being deported if caught and could not afford to doubt the man's belligerent humor. The man agreed that Sabr would have his visa for a fee of $1,200 a year, paid in installments every three months, and would continue working for Mr. Malek in the daytime while tending to some maintenance work at the sponsor's villa on his time off. In the hollow chill of winter, Sabr held his breath and paid his sponsor, who handed over his officiated visa.

He lamented the war in Syria deeply. He was still not accustomed to living away from his wife and now three children, and the cost of the visa was an additional expense he had to budget for. He tried to look for work in the evenings. Eager to impress his new sponsor, however, he sprang to answer his every call and command. He needed a trusting relationship with both his employer and his sponsor—a need surpassed only by that of providing for and spending time with his family. He worked endlessly to these aims.

When flowers began to blossom, it was time for his vacation. Though Mr. Edward approved his two-week leave, his sponsor's jokes turned to venom. He objected to Sabr leaving before he finished a list of renovations: laying tile in the bathroom, changing windows, fixing the roof ... And if the work order wasn't humiliating enough, he reminded Sabr that at any disobedience, he would withdraw his visa and have the police at his door by nightfall. Sabr felt defeated. He felt imprisoned. Even when crossing into warring Syria the three times he managed to visit his family, he was chained by another dictator. The year passed, and his visa needed to be renewed with no other option than the same devil.

On a cold morning before he began work, his wife called with news that froze his heart. Their youngest son, Ayham, had been running a fever for days and his face was yellow. They looked for hospitals, but the majority were destroyed in the war. Doctors finally diagnosed Ayham with leukemia and braced the family for cancer treatment.

Sabr rushed home to hold his son and carry him into the first rounds of treatment, reassuring his weak toddler that the radiation machines and wires were not scary. Ayham was treated for a year before the doctors admitted his condition was terminal. Sabr demanded a holiday from his sponsor, who responded with an order to have his bedroom painted in five colors, one for each wall. Sabr requested to cancel his *kafala* at the end of the year. The sponsor replied, "I know what to do."

After working at the construction site all day, Sabr peddled on the streets at night: vegetables, flowers, cigarettes, shoes ... no work was beneath him. When they sold Yasmeen's jewelry, he felt no shame. A strange humility took over him. On the road to Latakia, Sabr contemplated his options, but the war made everything desolate. The people left were like burning coals dropped in water. He tried to spend every moment with his son, but had to return to

Beirut. Before leaving on the last morning, Ayham called out to him, "*Baba*, take this scarf so you don't get cold. I love you, *Baba*." He hugged his father weakly, barely able to grip his jacket. Sabr could not see the road from Latakia to Beirut, blinded by his tears.

The Death

In the early morning, Sabr's phone rang. An officer with a commanding voice said that there was a problem with his visa. Sabr contemplated what malice his sponsor was plotting as he handed over his papers to an officer at the station. He implored them to tell him what the problem was. Why were his passport and visa being withdrawn? A stonewalling officer sent him to another station for investigations.

Sabr chased his papers through bureaucracy, and was told his visa had expired weeks ago and that his papers were being held to process his deportation. Confrontations with his sponsor ended with more insults and threats. Sabr tried explaining to an officer that his son had cancer and he needed to return. The man fired back, "Your son will die—it's not a problem! You Syrians give birth to a lot of kids. You add and you subtract. Now get out of my face!" With fists clenched, he struggled to grip his papers and will his numbing body to take action. His deadened feet shuffled to the hallway, where he gave up.

His crying was broken by a female officer. She pulled him to his feet, brought Sabr to her department and offered him water. She listened sympathetically, followed up on his papers, and guided him through the procedural mud. When Sabr was told his papers would be finalized in ten days, he wanted to feel happy, but any joy felt locked up. He couldn't sleep, so he prayed endlessly. On the third evening, Sabr dreamt of Ayham, who said to him, "Bye, *Baba*. I waited for you, and you couldn't make it. But don't worry. My brother is coming and he is similar. I love you! Bye, *Baba*."

Sabr woke up to his phone ringing. When he answered, Yasmeen's father said to him, "My son." Sabr answered, "We are of God, and to Him we will return." He spoke to Yasmeen, who told him Ayham had fallen into a coma before dying and that she had seen children in worse condition. Sabr got up to pray. As he knelt for his last prostration, he submitted to his grief. Sabr thought about how he was unable to bury his son, or wash him, or pay his hospital bills, or hold him ever again. He recalled his son's eyes and vitality as he held his phone looking at pictures of him, the last one of his corpse. He was consoled that Ayham passed quickly to the hands of God, and that Yasmeen did not have to suffer any further, but his heart hurt so much that he beat on it to lessen the pain. He felt his son's kisses, and how he bid him farewell with the scarf that Sabr could not bring himself to take off.

From Beirut to Latakia

The roads are not new to me, but this is the first time I want the trip home to take forever. I even wish that I don't ever arrive. I stand at the door for a while, wondering how to go inside without my youngest son there. I feel nervous, as if life is no longer real.

For days I wonder when I will wake up from this dream. Then I think about Ali and Mahmoud, how they love their brother and love sharing their favorite stories of him to make us laugh. I think about their school and their future, the debts that are drowning me, the debts that follow me from Syria to Lebanon and back. The cost of living is impossible to keep up with.

I have to provide for my family. Besides God, they have no one to support them except me. I had to return to Lebanon, and since my visa is gone, I have no option but to enter illegally. The smugglers are some of the cruelest people I've ever had to pay. But I have to return to Beirut, the city that offers me stability but which is also torture. Beirut protects me from the war and is the best place where I can protect my family.

The Explosion

In Lebanon, I live in Ain el-Mreisseh. I arrive home from work a little after five in the evening, as usual. I shower and think about dinner. Everything seems normal. Suddenly, the ground shakes, and a very loud thud reverberates from the sea, as if a massive concrete building has imploded. No sooner do I ask God if this is an earthquake than the most spectacular explosion shatters my window, breaks down my front door, and knocks over the chairs in my kitchen. I'm shocked, unable to understand what is happening, so I look out my window. Glass and screams fill the streets. It's a strange sight, as if all of Beirut is shedding tears and blood together.

I don't wait for the elevator. I run down the stairs to check on my employers and colleagues. Some of their front doors are blown off, too. I think of our neighbor's newborn who sleeps under a window and rush to the ground floor to ask about her. Thank God they moved her bed just the day before. Everyone seems to be in good health, but glass and aluminum is everywhere. From the eighth floor balcony of the building across the street, we hear a woman screaming that her father is bleeding. Her cries for help move our feet before we have time to think.

Their building has a large metal gate, plaited like jail bars. It had been blown off three hinges and tilted onto a corner. We try to crouch through a small gap, and as I do, the gate begins to fall on me. I try to back away, but it falls faster and lands on my legs with such force that I almost pass out. More people rush to help me. They manage to lift a part of it, but my legs are still stuck because a thin metal bolt has burst through both my legs, nailing me to the gate. I don't know how they manage to slide me out. It is a miracle how they carry me. I keep screaming, "The man upstairs is bleeding! Help him please! He's old and he's bleeding!" Then I pass out because I, too, am bleeding heavily.

I regain consciousness an hour later and find myself in the corridor of an emergency floor in a Beirut hospital. There is pandemonium everywhere and the smell of blood is spreading frighteningly. The doctors and nurses are in a state of extreme confusion. My feet are bleeding terribly. The pain is very severe, and from time to time I feel violent dizziness. After a lot of struggle, one of my friends is able to draw the attention of a young doctor, who says the hospital is in a critical situation.

"But the man is bleeding badly," my friend explains. The doctor comes forward, performs some first aid and says to me. "This needs stitches to stop the bleeding. You'll be taken in for X-rays. Your legs have several fractures, and you'll need surgery."

Hours pass, and though I am in great pain, there is an even greater pain in my chest. My leg is broken, but my heart won't stop bleeding. I'm obliged to think about my financial situation and my family. My only dream is to provide them with a new life after all they've suffered all these years. Besides God, they have no one else to support them. I think about my debts, and how they're accumulating, whether I'm in Beirut or Syria. I wonder what to tell my wife, who's in her fourth month of pregnancy. How will I provide for my sons when I am unable to walk? As I lie there, I pray for the souls around me. I let the tears fall as I think of all my sons. All these thoughts dry up my body.

Doctors begin to care about me somewhat, asking me questions, but I am unable to answer. In these difficult thoughts, my phone rings. It is my four-months-pregnant wife. I hang up, hoping this will signal to her that I'm alive. She calls again and again. I gather all my strength, and try to speak in a normal voice. Yasmeen asks calmly, "Are you OK? There is news on television that Beirut has had a big explosion. Please reassure me about you."

I tell her it's just the tears in my eyes. I haven't been injured, my health is fine, but one of my friends is hurt, and I'm with him at the hospital, as his situation is slightly critical. She doesn't believe me, "Open a video call. Let me see you so that I can believe it."

I have to be firm but gentle at the same time, so I respond, "Don't you believe me? Here I am, talking to you., and they don't allow any cameras here anyway. Please be reassured, if even slightly," and I end the call. I return to the excruciating pain. The nurses take me to a room with a man in his fifties. His injuries are so many, and so critical. I can see death reaching his eyes, this poor man. I try to calm myself.

The Hospital

My wife keeps calling, and I keep reassuring her that I'm fine. The doctors tell me that I have fractures in my right leg and that my left leg is broken in two places and needs surgery and months to recover. I think about my family and their future. I feel like I have let down my children. I can no longer endure the lying, and after four days I tell Yasmeen, trying not to shock her with sadness.

The doctors wait nine days for the swelling in my legs to reduce so they can operate. The pain is so terrible that I need strong sedatives to sleep. A few friends visit me to distract me, but I'm more preoccupied when a nurse gives me the coronavirus test. The next morning, they wheel me to the waiting room for surgery and draw the curtains. I hear an older woman moaning in pain in the far corner of the room. It makes my heart sink.

I ask a nurse about her condition, and I'm told that she urgently needs an operation, so I ask if I can give up my turn to hasten hers. If I wait, they say, then I will suffer like she is suffering now, as my painkillers will fade and I am not allowed any more before the operation.

I answer, "If your conscience allows you to hear the screams of this poor woman, my conscience does not. Please give her my turn, and I will bear the pain."

Two and a half hours pass, and my pain is severe. They finally wheel me inside. The anesthetic injection is a sleep I haven't felt in years. I wake up in the intensive care unit. I don't feel any pain. They take me back to my room, and I ask the nurses about the lady, but they won't tell me her name or anything about her. Two days later, the doctors discharge me from the hospital after giving me a list of medicines that I don't have the money for. I continue on medication for six weeks without moving from my bed, and then I have a follow-up treatment once a month. I return home pregnant, immobile, unable to put my feet on the ground. I'm able to ask about the woman's father who I tried to help, and I learn that he is in good health.

No Title

Mr. Malek is very generous with me, and I am very grateful, but I am afraid to imagine what a burden I am on him. It is not my habit to tell anyone—even my wife—that I need money, or that I don't have anything. My mother says that as a child, I would never run to her crying if one of my brothers refused to let me play with his toys. I was always patient and self-sufficient, never a nagging child.

A friend gave me the number of one of the charities helping victims of the blast. I call them hoping they can help me. A young man asks me several questions, and I answer all of them. The last question comes:

"What is your nationality?" I tell him that I am a Syrian and he apologizes, saying that the association only helps the Lebanese. I answer, "Does this explosion distinguish between the Syrian—the Egyptian—the Bangladeshi?" Again he apologizes and I close the line. My usual thoughts chase me, even though I can't move.

I don't know how the months go by. Every day I feel anxious and heartbroken, thinking about my wife on the verge of giving birth. I ask one of my younger brothers to move Yasmeen and my children back to my parent's house in Aleppo, and to sell the washing machine, the refrigerator, and what we have in Latakia. He asks me if I need money, and I tell him no, that I want to buy new electrical appliances as a surprise for my wife and children, since they are now residing in my family's home. He manages to sell them, and I make him promise not to tell anyone. He gives the money to my wife, saying, "Your husband has sent you the childbirth expenses."

A few days later, my wife gives birth to a healthy boy who we name Adham. This is the only moment of joy during these months, these years, through everything I experienced before and after the explosion—an incredible explosion that killed humans before destroying stone.

The months that pass me by are painful. And so I wait, I wait for deliverance from God, hoping that my mental and physical wounds will heal. This is my current condition, without change, to this day.

Written by Hala Srouji
Story contributed anonymously

Afterword

Sabr's leg would not heal properly, even after several months of physical therapy. His mental state was overburdened by guilt. He felt like he had exhausted the generosity of his former employer and failed in his role as provider for his family. He searched for work everywhere, reached out to every contact he had, and stood under bridges where illegal refugees scrounged for a day's work. He endured countless hours of demeaning physical labor for peanuts.

When the weather turned warm and the sea beckoned him to swim, he received another devastating phone call: his eighty-seven-year-old father had passed away in his sleep. First his son, then his father. Both died in his absence. Sabr could not bear being far from his family any longer.

The driver who agreed to smuggle him into Syria demanded $450, and another $100 to bribe the checkpoints. Sabr sold his small dining table, two chairs, and a single bed and mattress. His clothes no longer fit his gaunt frame, and he distributed his few remaining belongings among his friends. Wearing his leather jacket in the middle of August, he imagined himself a corpse along the road from Beirut to Damascus. Only the embrace of his family brought him back to life.

Doctors in Syria found that his operation had been poorly executed, and corrective surgery was conducted. Since then, Sabr has applied to the Ministry of Public Works and is still waiting for a response. He visits a nearby psychologist as often as his budget will allow.

Sabr prays for the crises in Lebanon and Syria to end. He plans to migrate wherever it's feasible, though he always concludes that Beirut remains the most practical option.

What If?

What would've happened if Omar and Sally had made different decisions that day? Did they have any control over how things turned out? Could anything have mattered at all? Why them? Why not them?

Omar could've been at the office that day. Rather, he should've been there. But something beyond his comprehension took over him, a heaviness unlike anything he had ever felt before. He needed out. But why did he decide to go to that specific branch of FabricAID, the secondhand clothes collection-and-distribution company he had founded back in 2017? The enterprise, originally a personal initiative manned exclusively by Omar, now boasted several stores throughout Beirut. Yet somehow Omar had chosen to head to the one in Gemmayze.

Sally was there, too. They were coworkers and friends. They had originally met through her sister-in-law, who also happened to be Omar's best friend. Sally had only joined the FabricAID team as a retail stylist a few months prior. Her 2020 New Year's resolution was to find a job she really enjoyed, and when an offer to work with a seller of vintage clothing popped up on Instagram, she knew she'd found it. It was thus with much enthusiasm that she went about this first day back at work, with the country partially out of COVID quarantine once again. In fact, Sally had an intuition that day that was the polar opposite to the anxiety engulfing Omar. In her mind, the day would be great.

Why did Omar choose to stick around that day? What pushed him to miss meetings, something he had never done before? It was a day of firsts that he could not explain.

But catching up with Sally was so pleasant. Despite the time that elapsed since they had first met, it felt like they were getting to know each other all over again. It all started with an innocent query regarding a colleague of theirs getting engaged. How could they celebrate?

Sally picked up the phone and called every venue in Beirut, as she was itching to get things going. But everything was closed, still affected by the crisis and the virus. This was just hours before these places would be wiped out. But they did not know that. No one could have.

What would you have done had you known what would happen that day? If you had been the only one aware of what would take place?

But let us not digress. There is no point in dwelling on maybes. It happened.

Before it happened, Sally was still trying and failing to plan a happy evening. After that, the pair kept talking. And talking. And talking. No less than five hours were spent conversing, stolen moments of bliss before the blast.

Lunchtime came and passed. Then hunger hit. Sally considered leaving the shop to fetch food from the nearby Sandwich w Nos before settling on ordering in. One more decision led by factors unknown that could have been fatal had things gone differently.

The food came.

One bite.

Two bites.

The sound of a plane, loud. Sally thought it was a passenger airline, crashing.

Picture this: the shop, small, hangers and clothes delimiting the passageways. The pair, each sitting in a chair.

Sally was frozen above her salad, fork in hand. The hope of a good day vanished from her mind in a heartbeat.

Omar, a man of action, can't stay in place. The hold on his throat since morning is now suffocating. *Must go check. Must reassure Sally.* Up he stands and out he goes to the balcony, only to be greeted by a scream. A voice calling his name.

Sally, still frozen in place, her hands in front of her eyes, fingers slightly spread so her gaze could catch his. Ever since she was a child, her biggest fear had always been that of losing her sight. And now she felt that her eyes were in danger. Memories of her parents' tales of the civil war. If you hear a plane, stay inside. The blast isn't far behind.

Omar, pragmatic. Omar, convinced this was just a bomb like so many others he had heard before. Convinced the danger was behind them, far away, already avoided. But he listened to Sally, to comfort her maybe. What if he had stood his ground for two seconds longer?

The shop was facing the port, with only one tall building between them. Omar saw smoke coming from the port. He knew the sound had come from there. But it was far. And it was done. He could've brushed her off.

But he turned his back to the smoke and took a step inside.

See? He was fine.

Then his other foot hit the next tile.

The clock read 6:07 PM sharp.

Where were you when it happened? Did you hear it? Did you feel it? Did you see it?

At first, they saw nothing at all. They couldn't really say they heard anything either. But they felt it. The pressure. Heavy. Suffocating. Breathtaking.

Omar came to. Darkness surrounded him. He could not move. Was he…?

A voice. His name. Sally.

Sally felt the pressure engulfing her. She kept her hands firmly in front of her eyes. In her mind, death was only a matter of time, but she needed to make sure her eyes would make it if she did.

And when it all came to a stop, she called out for Omar. When he heard her voice, two things became clear. One: she was alive. Two: so was he. He pushed with all his strength to free himself from the wooden beam that had trapped him, a beam that only minutes ago had been part of the ceiling. Braving the dust-induced darkness, he made his way through the carnage of furniture and clothes.

The pair would later find out that many items had been thoroughly marked with their blood. Because blood had very much been shed. Sally made her way to a mirror, the one item of furniture standing tall amid the chaos. It was covered with dust, but once wiped up it was good as new, defying destruction by its unwavering immobility.

What Sally saw in that mirror was her once curly hair, now straightened, matted by the sheer amount of blood that covered it. This was made even more obvious by her formerly white blouse, now tainted red all over. But Sally didn't care about what she saw. What she cared about most was the fact that she even saw at all. She could see. Everything else would be fine, somehow.

In adversity, we humans tend to have our convictions put to the test. We often fantasize about how we'd behave in a crisis. But don't you wonder how true these thoughts turn out to be when faced with reality?

This train of thought struck Omar the most. When they finally left the shop, he stood in place. Baffled, speechless, heartbroken. Destruction surrounded him, and all he could think of was Beirut. Before his family even crossed his mind, he was obsessed with the state of his city. He always knew he loved Beirut, but the pain he felt at that moment was more devastating than he could have ever imagined.

Another conviction of his was reassured that day: when faced with such a situation, he would help others before helping himself. This much was true. Omar led Sally to individuals in need, assisting them as best they could. One woman wanted to offer them coffee as thanks. They declined and left, not wanting to witness the look on her face when she eventually realized that she no longer had a kitchen.

What went through Sally's mind was different. She had no prior convictions to test through these trials. Instead, something awoke in her that had long been buried right under the surface: faith. She had not prayed in years, but something was giving her the strength to go on, despite the fear and the pain.

She felt the need to get moving. They marched through a sea of the wounded and frightened who were navigating away from the port, walking straight ahead yet wandering aimlessly, deported from the rubble that was once their homes.

The pair's wounds needed tending to, but the hospitals … Have you ever watched a war movie where the victims were led to be treated on the field? Beds overfilled, mangled limbs rivalling for attention with exposed tissue, doctors and nurses scrambling about, hands full but not much better than useless? Such were the hospitals of Beirut on the evening of August 4, 2020.

Our pair was fortunate to be able to walk on functioning limbs with heads still thinking straight. But their wounds remained numerous and deep. They had to be cleaned and stripped of glass. They had to be mended. Sally needed surgery on her hand, as the tendon had almost snapped. There was no anesthesia. But yet again, something out there helped contain her screams.

Like any other day, August 4th came to an end. After it, new days came, bringing new choices along with them.

Omar could not sleep that night. After his realization about his deep love for Beirut, he was itching to help. He went out and volunteered alongside hundreds of others, armed only with brooms and determination. After some time, Omar deferred back to his enterprise, FabricAID, and expanded it to FabricRelief, to form teams to better assist in cleanup and food distribution. The initiative felt like a call from the past, taking him back to how FabricAID started in the first place: to fill a need. In late 2016, Omar had some clothes to donate and asked his family what to do with them. They suggested giving them to the building's concierge. The concierge, however, had no use for the family's clothes and, though he accepted such donations graciously, then had to find ways to dispose of them. So instead, Omar went to a poor neighborhood near his home and started asking people there what they needed in terms of size, color, fabric, style, trying to match their requests with his and his friends' donations. He was quickly overwhelmed. He worked and studied full-time back then, and tried to delegate the task to local NGOs. But he could tell they couldn't handle the charge, so he took it upon himself to start FabricAID.

This time around, people needed help more than ever. Omar had nothing holding him back from giving it his all. He had lost his car and his home, but he chose to focus on what he had left, on his country, and on what mattered most—its people, united under one cause. Just like FabricAID, FabricRelief was Omar's way of being part of the solution when the problem came knocking at his door.

As for Sally, her choices were limited. The wound in her hand forced her to remain in bed, after which she could only distribute meals. Despite not having the same convictions as Omar, she too felt the need to go out and help, feeling restless when bedbound. But her newly found faith comforted her further in those trials.

What would have happened had there not been a pandemic? Had people been roaming the streets of Gemmayze and Mar Mikhael by the hundreds, as they usually did?

If you're like Sally, you would cite divine intervention. If you're like Omar, you'd believe things just happen and we can only control what we do about them. But you're you.

What would you have done had you been in their place?

Written by Carmina Khairallah
Story contributed by Omar Itani and Sally Khadra

Glass

I t's been more than six weeks now, and the days are still hot—not just hot—sticky, and too close. Michelle and Marie crank up the AC as soon as they are back in the car and pull out into a city known but now fleetingly, yet repeatedly, unfamiliar. It snags the eye at intervals. Building facades have changed and the streets remain in chaos. Rules were always bendable here—a quick slip the wrong way down a one-way thoroughfare more than acceptable—but now the rules have been inverted: some streets run the opposite course, others are closed, barricaded by debris or fears of building collapse. Patience is required to navigate this new terrain. But today, with the AC on high, this patience is easy to find, and this time in the car, one of the last trips they'll make together, is something they cherish. In a bag behind the passenger seat is the item they came into the city to pick up: a glass carafe—so dark it is almost black.

The carafe, snug in its bubble wrap, has its own tale. This city they are now making an eastward exit from is familiar to it too—it is soldered from its parts. Its desirability as a possession isn't in its beauty or craftsmanship, though those things are certainly there on some level; it is in its origins, in what it physically encapsulates. This carafe is made of blast glass—it is a vessel made from a city that shattered.

It is 6:05 PM on August 4, and life is normal. Ziad Abi Chaker is in his studio just off Sami al-Solh Street. The working day is closing out. Three kilometers away, Michelle is with another friend, drinking wine from paper cups in a closed café. On the roof of the building, a man and a woman down cold beer. All across the city, the people—skin filmed in sweat from a long, hot Beirut summer day in the middle of a pandemic—are slipping out of the toil and into the evening's short respite. Later, they'll come back to those closing moments, recount them second by second, hold them up to the light like a glass splinter extracted from the skin and inspect them, turning them around, marveling, hardly able to fathom that such normalcy, such comfort and safety, were ever integral to them. The windows through which they watch the world, the AC on high for sweet relief, are still innocuous transparencies.

Two minutes later, everything changes. Windows are no longer windows. Ziad, almost five kilometers from the blast site, though he doesn't know what's happened yet, descends into Badaro, an art deco neighborhood where boho chic cafés and bars line the streets, and law firms keep offices in more modern towers nearby. When he reaches the street, the sound of his footsteps is strangely altered. Crunch. Glass. There is glass underfoot.

In the hours that follow the explosion, radios and televisions and buzzing phones make clear what has happened and its magnitude. There are bloodied people everywhere, and three hospitals are totally out of action. Cars with shattered windows struggle to get out of the city to other health facilities. The sun sinks into the Mediterranean, like it does every evening, but that night is different—the darkness somehow bidden and appropriate as the weight of what's happened becomes clear, and families realize that loss and grief are now their lot. Across the world, hearts connected to this sliver of land contract, breaths are held as voices are awaited on the other end of the phone, the same question is repeated again and again:

"Are you OK?"

Ziad makes these rounds of calls—answering those who ask, checking on those he needs to check on—but already, even with the shock still reverberating, another thought is percolating as the shards continue to crunch.

Ziad's self-professed passion in life is garbage. He's built his career on it. He's been working in trash in Lebanon for the better part of two decades, battling to make recycling mainstream, but his country—which he chose to return to after going to university in New Jersey—remains obstinately committed to land-fills as its main mechanism for trash management. It is difficult not to despair at this stubbornness: Beirut's landfills are overflowing and closing and disputed. In 2015, garbage went uncollected for weeks as the city ran out of places to put it. It piled high in the streets. And it stank. It stank so much that thousands of people made placards and marched to the parliament building in Downtown, their message to the country's politicians unambiguous: "YOU STINK."

So, on Aug. 4, 2020, while two friends leave a café hand-in-hand and attempt to walk beyond the destruction, and a man and a woman, beers abandoned, tend to a bleeding neighbor, and a city wails and reels, Ziad starts to think about the Beirut municipality; Ziad starts to think about the capital's overflowing landfills; Ziad looks at his destroyed city and thinks about trash.

Despite the protests five years earlier, very little has changed. Space was found. The trash mountains left the street. And Ziad continued his work. The bottle banks of his company, Cedar Environmental—not the state's bottle banks—stand on street corners. He recycles the glass and sells products—jugs, carafes, glasses, lamps—made from it. He also takes the discarded plastic bags of his country—where supermarkets bag and double-bag groceries with abandon—and turns them into a durable construction material known as eco board. His plants sort waste, and he's not alone. There are other organizations crusading and fighting to reduce Lebanon's dependence on landfill, but they are a minority, and the state is an adversary, not an ally.

So, when windows shattered for miles at 6:07 PM on August 4, 2020, leaving some 5,000 tons of glass on the streets, Ziad knew very quickly that he would be in a race against the state if he didn't want all that waste—250 truckloads worth, as it turned out—to end up in landfill.

On August 5, after months of relative quiet during lockdown and corona-virus restrictions, the city is oddly vibrant. People flock to the streets, moving slowly and carefully, reaching for each other out of shared experience. They take stock of injuries, damages, and losses. Embraces—the need for touch obliterat-ing fears of virus spread—are full of tears and often relief. And amid the throng there is only one sound, or so it seems on that day: glass—cracking underfoot, shards clinking noisily as they are swept up, shattering further as dustpan loads are dropped into dumpsters.

Ziad mobilizes his team quickly. He has volunteers. He finds funding for trucks. He creates jobs as they are needed. And they sweep and gather and collect. Glass. They know what to do with it. They know how to take what is broken and transform it into something new, something that can be used.

Ziad's first assumption is that he will send his collected blast glass to the renowned and almost magical-sounding glass blowers of Sarafand. It makes sense. These are the artisans he's been working with for years, and they are, he believes, the only remaining commercial practitioners of this art in the country. But this plan quickly runs aground. There is simply too much glass, and it's being collected too quickly for the Sarafand blowers to process. The furnace in the southern town can only process 330 pounds of glass per day—more than enough capacity to handle what recyclable glass Ziad's company usually collects, but not nearly enough to process the glass from the explosion. So Ziad looks for alternatives.

He stumbles upon two other factories, Uniglass and Golden Glass, which have ovens with a much larger capacity. Both are at the other end of the country, in Tripoli. The discovery creates new possibilities for transforming salvaged glass. In the weeks that follow, some 140 tons of blast glass are transformed into *briqs*, jugs, and carafes in the companies' furnaces.

The products produced are not perfect—this is no pristine, high-quality, transparent crystal. Some of the collected glass is too impure, too mixed with other debris, and is instead sent to be used in cement. The carafes that take shape as the blowers exhale down long, thin metal straws into molten glass are gray-black, patterned by swirls and occasional bubbles. To some eyes they may even seem ugly. But when you hear the story of this glass, how it has been swept up from a devastated landscape, trucked northward, and transformed and reconfigured, it is the most beautiful dark glass in the world.

For a long time, Ziad has held a stand at the weekly Souq al-Tayeb market, a place where small-scale Lebanese producers and artisans gather to sell their products. The market itself is located in Mar Mikhael, one of the worst-damaged areas in the explosion. When it resumes business within weeks of the blast, it comes as a comfort to many, an acknowledgement that life can continue, albeit likely with trepidation. Ziad's stall is in the back right-hand corner. It is here that he first displays his vessels made from glass recycled from the blast, at the market's first week back after the explosion. It is here that Michelle comes, accompanied by Marie, to select one item from Ziad's collection. The carafe she is looking for is intended as a gift for her in-laws some thousands of miles from a shattered Beirut.

Michelle has spent so many moments over the past several weeks thinking about glass, traumatized by it, astounded over it. She vividly remembers all that glass flying in at her. She remembers that, and many other things too, and sometimes she awakes in a panic, or can't get to sleep at all. So, in their Mount Lebanon home, in the small hours, as her husband, John, and son sleep, as the friends from the city who they've sheltered after the explosion sleep, as her two adopted dogs sleep, she scrolls through her phone, wondrous at how her own body escaped physically unscathed.

She makes a mental list of all the places she could have been at 6:07 PM that day. It's a list she knows she's not alone in making. Everyone has been doing it—Beirut in the aftermath of the blast is a town of half a million miracles:

"If I'd been two feet this way…"

"If I'd left five minutes later…"

Michelle doesn't live in the city, but she does work there, at a Lebanese NGO not far from the port. Her office windows shattered across her desk, but she'd left an hour or so earlier. Countless friends live in the vicinity—in Geitawi, Gemmayze, Ashrafieh—and she could feasibly have been in any of their homes. Or she might have been on the road, heading out of the city past the giraffe-like sentries that seem to stand guard at the port's container terminal toward the mountains above Beirut, where the humidity mercifully drops as you gain elevation—but she isn't. Instead, she meets a friend for a late afternoon chat in a Geitawi café. The friend needs to pass by her own place of work, another coffee shop, this one in Gemmayze, and even though the walk between the two places is no more than fifteen minutes, the sweltering heat prompts Michelle to say, "My car's nearby. I'll drive you."

Once in Gemmayze, still chattering, they park the car and enter the café together. It is closed because of coronavirus concerns, so they are alone. The space is long and narrow, and two sides are completely made of glass. They are still talking when the explosion cuts into the conversation with its great inhalation of breath—a sound that will mean that low-flying jets, rolling thunder, or anything similarly deep and ominous and growing will drive both women to take cover for years to come. Then the world is airborne glass.

Michelle thinks about this, and she comes to credit glass with her survival—or at least a type of glass: the tempered kind. In the closed café at 6:07 PM, just 750 meters from the port, the two glass sides are blown in, but instead of transforming into dagger-like shards, the panes shatter into small, much less lethal cubes. Sleepless, Michelle wonders who is responsible for this. She ponders the individuals who developed this safety glass and those who made the decision to install it at that particular shop. She writes an Instagram post saluting the kind of care and love that creates and chooses to use something safer, just in case … just in case the unlikely happens, just in case someone unknown to you, somewhere in the future, might need that extra protection. There is comfort in thinking about those humans who act with consideration toward people they've never met and may never know. It's a kind of salve in the face of its polar opposite: the kind of negligence that leaves tons and tons of ammonium nitrate stacked haphazardly in a warehouse just meters from the city's commercial and residential areas. The Beirut blast, as people will come to call it, happened at 6:07 PM on August 4, 2020. But it could have happened at any minute of any day or night during the previous six years. Our city was a time bomb—maybe it still is.

Glass. Six weeks after the explosion the little cubes still show up in unlikely places—no one realizes it yet, but they will continue to do so for years. Michelle fishes them out of pockets, the corners of her handbag, and holds them up to the light. Glass. During the passing weeks, the sound of glass has retreated somewhat, and life, irrepressible, has pushed forward. Family circumstances quickly and a little unexpectedly expedite the end of Michelle's time in Lebanon. She's been here for four years, working with a Lebanese NGO she first joined while still living in California. She isn't ready to leave. She's uncomfortable departing while the city that has been her home, and so many of the people in it, remain so damaged and uncertain of the future. It is excruciating to go, but also impossible to stay.

She starts to pack up her house—all the physical memories of bonds and friendships and hurts and hopes. She follows Ziad on Instagram. She knows of his eco board. Needing a crate for shipping, she orders the panels from him, and her husband hammers and nails them together. Their life in Lebanon will journey to California, held by the recycled waste produced here.

It is in this crate that she and Marie will place the black carafe—a fragment of the 125 tons of glass from the blast that Ziad and his team have transformed into glassware. Marie, with decades of experience working in antiquities, takes responsibility for securing it. She unwraps the bubble wrap and repacks the carafe with both expertise and love. She then nestles it into the crate. It will travel in that crate down from Mount Lebanon and through the shattered city of its birth. It will pass into a port in disarray, the driver of the truck on which it transits likely feeling his chest tighten again as he steers past the blasted grain silos and twisted metal of devastated warehouses.

Months later, the crate will arrive in California. Michelle and her husband will lever the nails out and crack it open, reminding themselves that there is no guarantee everything survived the journey. But it has. The carafe has. Soon they will take it, this piece of rebuilt wholeness from a city recklessly, deplorably destroyed, and gift it to her mother-in-law. And into it she will decant, over the years to come, bottle after bottle of wine—some Lebanese, some Californian, some from other vineyards in other places. And family and friends will, time and again, pick it up and pour it, some conscious but many unaware that their hands, as they meet over a dinner table, are caressing a tiny, reconstituted, whole and functional part of a city striving to understand what it can be and how it, too, can remake itself, in a country where hope is embodied by people like Ziad, the glassblowers, and those who went to the streets with brooms and swept up the shards.

Written by Niamh Fleming-Farrell
Story contributed by Ziad Abichaker and Michelle Klewer

Crawa's Home, *Too*

Despite her size, she was a young soul, happy to be alive and exploring. Over at the pen, she waggled and pounced about on all fours. I saw her soft, black velvet coat, her glimmering brown eyes, and I knew that she was going to be my friend. She was my black crow: gentle, misunderstood, but oh so sweet. I named her Crawa.

Crawa and I developed a very special bond over the years. We had our own language; she signed to me with only her eyes, and what magical eyes she had. Despite all that has happened, she still signs with the same genuine love that she did all those years ago. We've had to make budget cuts, and her dry food is not as tasty as what she was used to, but she's a good girl; she doesn't complain. She doesn't get new toys as often, but we go on more walks. She's also happier these days because I spend more time at home. She's always so happy to see me in my studio. She loves watching me paint ...

But that day, that day was different.

I was in my studio, mixing my paint, and my brush kept darkening my lines. Crawa was sitting in a corner, and that was very unlike her. She's usually sitting by me, watching the lines as they curve on the canvas. I always wondered if she feels the same rush of the bristles fanning, sending their vibrations through the handle and into my wrist and fingers.

I looked at her and smiled. I signed to her: I'll be heading over to Rosalie's for dinner tonight. She turned around herself and sat.

Crawa; Good Girl. Daddy; Treat.

She looked at me and smiled, then dropped her head between her paws, resting it on the cold marble floor. She looked up at me with her twinkling eyes and smiled again. You know I can't resist that look, I signed. I headed over to the treat cabinet and came back to find her sitting up, ever so politely, waiting patiently for her treat. She's such a good girl.

Crawa. Good Girl. Daddy. Thank you.

Watching Paul get ready always elicited anxiety. Crawa would do everything in her power to either keep him there or convince him to take her with him. Today, as he walked towards his dresser to brush his hair, she followed him, squeezed herself between his legs, and rolled over belly-up on the ground.

Daddy. Crawa. Belly Rub. Good Girl.

Paul couldn't resist those eyes. He crouched down over her and gave her a belly rub; her hind paw kicked in erratic joy. He smiled at her softly and headed into the bathroom for a final check. Hair combed. Shirt on. Collar neat. He was ready to make his way to Rosalie's. As he turned towards the door, he found Crawa patiently waiting there with her leash in her mouth. When Paul made it to the door, she dropped it in front of him. He knelt down in front of her, ruffled her fur and signed: *Aww, I wish I could, Crawa, but this dinner is for humans. I already told you. I promise that tomorrow we'll go for a long walk, just you and me.*

As the door closed behind Paul, Crawa's head slowly sank between her paws and she let out a little whine. The clock struck 5:00 PM. The street was usually packed at this hour, and that day was no different. In fact, that day was one of two days of freedom. The whole country was on lockdown for what seemed like a century, and the government had given its tired citizens two days to go and run their essential errands before another period of confinement went into effect. The street was busy during rush hour, packed, loud with exhaust pipes sputtering and spitting black fumes, hands passionately gesturing and honking to wake the driver ahead and the angels above, people chatting, arguing, and laughing with others. Life—for a second, or so it seemed—had gone back to normal.

But Crawa wasn't feeling normal. The air was different that day. The echoes of people's chatter and laughter became increasingly nervous, almost manic, and Crawa's ears pointed upward, flexed forward then back, as if making a precise incision in the air above her head. She had felt the air thickening as she carefully walked around the house, examining each room for possible shelter. She ran to the front door and started barking, crying for help.

On high alert, she paced from one room to another, her ears pulling back as she stopped at every window, stared into the distance, and let out a single bark.

Daddy. Home. Now. Please.

Daddy. Danger. Home Please.

Daddy. Crawa. Scared.

Daddy. Crawa. Good Girl. Scared.

Crawa's barking carried through and echoed up the stairwell to reach Rosalie's door and knock frantically, but that is where it always stayed. Beyond the door, people spoke differently. It was quiet. 6:00 PM was not a special time. Noise was not overwhelming. Noise stayed at the door.

When Rosalie came into the world, Paul felt as though she had made her way through the universes, and into their family, just for him.

She was the last-born daughter, who, like Paul, didn't experience the morning birds chirping, the crash of an ocean wave, or their neighbor's godawful violin practice. Although Rosalie would eventually get a hearing aid and rely on reading lips to communicate with others, for the longest time she and Paul were the only ones who understood each other; they could plot, and keep everyone else out of their plans. Paul would motion to Rosalie from behind the arc that separated the bedrooms from the living room and kitchen, where their mother would be doing the dishes. She would tiptoe behind him until they just reached their mother's apron. Paul would point left, Rosalie would head right, and they would proceed to tickle their mother, whose shocked laughter would vibrate through the walls of the kitchen. Paul and Rosalie would hurry out before their mother could spray them with water again.

Growing up, Paul's favorite part of every day was making Rosalie laugh. He would watch her nose crinkle, a vein in her forehead pop out, her cheeks flush, her hands land emphatically and repeatedly on the tops of her thighs. Then she'd make her great escape and shuffle out of the room to get some air. Rosalie's laughter rang down the halls, carrying her joy in waves down into the streets. Paul had always been a prankster, but that was not all that he was. Underneath all of his harmless practical jokes, was a love like no other. His heart fit his entire family, and he had always known that he had space for one more.

The dinner table looked lovely, rich in nutritious foods: a rice salad with chicken breast, pasta, fava beans, and vegetables cut up in perfect bite-size, and a beef potato stew. It was all very neatly presented for our eyes to feast on before our rumbling bellies. I could always rely on Rosalie to prepare a big meal for everyone. She thinks everyone is as active as she is. I smiled and nodded at her as she served me some chicken salad. My mother and father sat across from us, smiling despite the fact that we were having dinner in the humid heat of August, with absolutely no ventilation or cooling. Our dinner conversations had circled around three main topics as of late: the spread of COVID-19, the economic collapse, and the intolerable power cuts that dipped the hot summer nights of Beirut in total, humid darkness. And as if life hadn't gotten hard enough, mosquitos made their way into every home as Beirut's windows kept their arms open.

For reasons we couldn't explain, Rosalie and I felt anxious. It was as though the walls were radiating and pulsing into the structure of the building. The floor tiles under our feet buzzed and sent vibrations into our legs. The air around us felt tight, as though it were pushing against our skin. Something didn't feel right.

Rosalie and I looked at each other. We were both feeling it. I looked to my parents to see if they noticed what we were noticing. Mom and dad were still chewing on their salads and conversing. Suddenly, they both looked to the window, their eyes wide in horror. They looked to each other and held hands, Mom's nails digging into Dad's hands

The unfamiliar pressure in the air eventually pushed so hard against our skin that we held on to each other's hands simultaneously. Then the world dropped and started seizing. I watched the dining room's chandelier move from one side to the other, along with the walls, the floors, the doors. Rosalie and I shared a look of terror and made our way to the hallway. Our parents followed. We all huddled together and waited, braced for impact.

The air in the room checked out, saying it would be better off without us.

The whole house went reeling. Rosalie's delicious meal was strewn across the dining room floor, mixed with broken glass and window frames. Every piece of art that decorated her living room held on by a thread for dear life. Dust and debris filled the air. My parents covered each other's heads with their arms, their elbows over each other's ears. I wonder how loud it must have been.

My head hurt.

I checked on Rosalie. She was shaken up, but thankfully had no injuries on her body, and neither did Mom and Dad. Mine were shallow cuts, nothing major. We weren't hurt. But then my back shuddered. I stood up and allowed what felt like ice water to pour down my spine. *Crawa!*

Daddy. Scared. Crawa. Danger. Help. Please.

Crawa. Lost. Daddy. Help.

Crawa. Good Girl. Daddy. Please.

Crawa. Good Girl. Daddy.

Daddy. Danger. Crawa. Hide.

Crawa. Good Girl. Crawa. Hide.

Crawa. Good Girl.

Crawa. Want. Belly Rub.

Crawa. Want. Food.

Crawa. Want. Water.

Crawa. Good Girl.

Daddy. Come. Please.

Crawa. Good Girl.

I walked a street I thought I knew. It was only later that I remembered that it looked nothing like it used to. My neighborhood was a sad gray-and-red pool of rubble, shards of glass, and injured neighbors. I was on a mission: to find Crawa. I knew Rosalie was looking too. *Don't forget to check the plastic waste disposal. She couldn't have gone far,* she texted me. Crawa is strong and resilient, but she's small and she was so scared, I could feel it. We're all much larger than she is, and we were terrified. Smoke and debris hovered over our heads, and ambulances flashed red and blue lights through the dark city, picking up one severely injured person after the other. I know for sure that I tried to call out to her, but I'm not certain that I sounded out her name: "Crawa!"

I spent the whole night looking for her. I knew she was waiting for me to come find her, but by the early hours of the morning, my blistered feet could no longer hold me. I had to rest. I had to find her. I had to know that she was alright. I hoped that she would forgive me for a few hours of sleep. It's all the same, or maybe it isn't. In the next few days, parents, children, fiancées, husbands, and wives would be looking for their loved ones too, but they won't know. They won't know if their loved ones were alive or dead or hurt or injured. They knew they had to find them, one way or another, but they couldn't lose hope, and neither could I.

I texted Rosalie and told her that I was going to continue my search for Crawa after a couple of hours of sleep. She then texted back assuring me that she got all the glass out of my mattress. What she didn't realize was that removing the shards from my mattress was not going to stop the piercing pain in my heart, knowing that I'd be sleeping without Crawa in the house.

Daddy. Scared. Crawa. Danger. Help. Please.
Crawa. Lost. Daddy. Help.
Crawa. Good Girl. Daddy. Please.
Crawa. Good Girl. Daddy.
Daddy. Danger. Crawa. Hide.
Crawa. Good Girl. Crawa. Hide.
Crawa. Good Girl.
Crawa. Want. Belly Rub.
Crawa. Want. Food.
Crawa. Want. Water.
Crawa. Good Girl.
Daddy. Come. Please.
Crawa. Good Girl.

I remember Rosalie's face when I brought *Crawa* home for the first time. She was over the moon when my energetic pup spun twice and lay down at her feet with her belly exposed.

"Auntie Rosalie" soon became the only other human Crawa trusted with food, playtime, and warm cuddles.

In the dark, desolate streets, the echoes of Crawa's barks floated into every home, but when they reached Paul's window, they waited for a second before somberly drifting away.

It was too hot. Every time I closed my eyes, her sweet face was right there. Every time. There she was, wagging her tail as soon as I got to the front door. I turned to sleep on my left side, and there she was, running towards me in the studio with her ball. That means I've been in there too long. Every time. There she was. Bringing her full food plate and dropping it at my feet because she hadn't seen me eat yet. I turned to my right. And there she was. Running down the street on our walks, then back to keep me motivated. I was too slow for her. I lay flat on my back, and every time a gust of humid, painful breeze swept by my foot, I would startle, hoping that maybe she found her way back home, and that she was just about to jump up on the bed and cuddle up against my chest, her soft fur tickling the sides of my face ...

I decided to get up and head into the kitchen. I made myself a cup of tea in the darkness. That night felt like the darkest night ever. I sat down by my kitchen window with my tea and waited, waited for a cool breeze to put out the burning in the pit of my stomach.

Crawa. Scared.

I wanted to stop going to the darker corners of my mind. I kept replaying the last time I saw her in my head. The way she looked at me at the door. The way she begged me to take her with me. She was such a good girl. *IS.* She *is* such a good girl. She can't be gone.

Crawa. Hungry.

Where could she have gone? She must be starving. I looked at her full bag of dry food in the kitchen. A hard ball formed in the center of my throat. I kept looking out the window, thinking of grabbing handfuls of her dry food and sprinkling it out on the street for her to find.

Crawa. Sad. Daddy. Play.

I walked into the living room and sat on the couch. Crawa's toys were all over the floor. I lay my head on the cushion and pulled out her favorite squeaky toy from behind it.

Come home, Crawa. Please.

Paul woke up a few hours later in a panic. He checked his phone. It was already eleven in the morning, and he had received multiple texts from Rosalie. *Come quick!* Paul sprung off the couch and put his shoes on. His socks were on an armchair, but he didn't have time. He was still shirtless and his eyes were still crusty but there was no time. He shot out of the doorway and slammed the air that used to be his door and climbed the steps two at a time. He knocked ferociously on the door, heaving, until Rosalie opened the door. And there she was: clean, delighted, and charging towards him. Rosalie watched in pride and a well of emotion she couldn't put into words as Paul and Crawa love-wrestled each other on the floor. Paul looked over to Rosalie, who stood there with the widest smile on her face.

Where did you find her? he signed. Rosalie smiled.

By the plastic waste disposal. You walk her by there every day. I woke up early and went to look there. She was hiding in a pool of plastic bottles.

Paul smiled and cuddled Crawa.

Thank you, he signed.

Don't mention it. She hesitated at first, but she was happy to come here for food and water.

Crawa's tail had never wagged this energetically, and Paul? Paul was OK. His and Rosalie's apartment had windows with broken arms and open doorways covered with nylon sheets to keep a semblance of privacy, perhaps just a suggestion, but in that very moment, Paul was OK. And Crawa, well, she was just Paul's black crow: gentle, misunderstood, but sweet.

Crawa. Brave. Good Girl. Treat.

Written by Youmna Bou Hadir
Story contributed by (Paul) Boghos Nazikian and Rosalie Nazikian

Uber Notes: A Journey of Survival

Golgotha has long been thought to be the site outside Jerusalem where Jesus was crucified. Golgotha, in Lebanese Arabic, is the chronic "Way of the Cross" that we have, once again, treaded.

6:03 PM After a surprisingly systematic day at work, reunited as a team after months in pandemic lockdown, I forge ahead with more normalcy and leave for my gym, located at the opposite end of Mar Mikhael. Though it's only a short distance away, I order an Uber so as not to be late, as I hate missing the warmup. The driver talks politics, COVID, the economic collapse. I pray there will not be traffic.

6:07 PM Inside the car, blanketed in glass shards, all I remember is the sound, resonating like the echo of ten thunderclaps at once. I find the courage to look up. In seconds, the city is swathed in smoke, covered in shades of gray. I plead to the Virgin loudly. *Ya 'Adra, ya 'Adra, ya 'Adra.*

As the crucifixion darkness begins to lift, I step outside the husk that the Toyota has become. Others too, aghast and speechless, emerge from their vehicles.

A woman is running, covered in blood, holding a newborn. I approach her, asking if the baby is fine.

"Yes," she answers, still walking. "I just want to get him out of here."

I find my phone, thrown from my hands into the front seat. After moments and connections lost in the impact, I receive my first message and start sending frenzied calls for help, for an ambulance. I try to type, "The woman! Her son!" I still think the damage is small scale.

My best friend Nicolas calls and explains that I should evacuate the scene, since it could blow up again.

The taxi driver is still checking the damages to his car; I ask him to walk with me somewhere safer, but he politely declines.

"This taxi is all I have," he says, as he hands me a tissue to wipe the blood off my face.

"*Hamdella as saleme.* Godspeed."

"*Alla maik amo.* May God be with you. Take care of yourself."

Carrying my two bags and my laptop, wearing just sandals, I start walking. First things first, I think to myself, let's go to Gemmayze. There's a Red Cross station there.

Only Gemmayze and Mar Mikhael, the contiguous streets that are the focus of Beirut's cosmopolitan and cultural life—its pubs, restaurants, art galleries, bookshops, French and Ottoman heritage haunts—are no longer there. The storied landmarks of our youth have been effaced by the heaps of rubble that repeat themselves in every direction. It is only now that I start to realize the enormity of what's happened. I hold my breath and refuse to cry.

In the immediate aftermath

Lines are alive again, and my phone is abuzz with messages from friends and family. I tell my mother I'm fine and turn off my phone to come up with a plan. The farther I walk, the more glass crunches under my feet, and the more zombie-like people emerge from flipped cars, imploring for help. Fires are everywhere, roads are blocked by the rubble from collapsed building, people's blood combining with dust and body parts to form the chastising smell of the dead and dying. *Bones, blood, plasma. Bones, blood, plasma. Bones, blood, plasma.* Motorcycles have been turned into ambulances, injured people of all ages clinging to the drivers. Those fortunate to remain alive will later have their wounds sutured with no anesthetic, under flashlight, in the parking lots of hospitals brought to their knees.

Amid the carnage, the debris, the destruction, the broken glass, a commanding voice rises, gradually, persistently, until finally I make sense of what is being said. A man is shouting my way, "Get in with this woman here, she will drive you to the nearest place you're trying to reach!"

I get into the front seat and look at the driver, a young hysterical mother waiting for a phone call about her children, who are supposedly at the family house near the MTC Touch building opposite Golgotha—ground zero. She is driving erratically, off-road over rocks and debris, her breathing labored and she keeps repeating the same thing: *Ma bi hemne gher wlede, bade bas wlede ykouno mneh. Ma bi hemne gher wlede, bade bas wlede ykouno mneh. I just want my children, I just want my children to be OK.*

I notice a small cross in her car, so I use faith, knowing that it helps, always.

"You are a believer, are you not? You love the ʿ*Adra*, and she abandons no mother who needs her." At first, my references to the Virgin do little to reassure the woman.

Her screams, relentless and raw, drown all the other voices, the demons in my head, and the din outside the car. *Ma bi hemne gher wlede. Ma bi hemne gher wlede. Ma bi hemne gher wlede.*

The woman calms down when I mention the ʿ*Adra* a second time. She asks for my name, looking at me as if she has only just realized I'm in the car.

Her husband calls. The children are with him. One has been slightly injured, but they are alive. I take the wheel once we finally pick them up; the kids are scared and shaken and need their mother's attention. And, just like magic, the woman is replaced by her doppelganger.

The overwrought, screaming woman, maddened by calamity, is now Tina, perfectly serene, composed and collected, in charge of the situation. She coaxes her children, cajoles them by whispering again and again, "Everything is going to be alright. Everything is going to be alright."

As we reach Tina's sibling's house near Badaro, I forget the debris and rubble, the glass and smoke. I forget the apocalypse surrounding us, above our heads, beneath our feet. Her repeated words, tenuous as they are, make me believe. I begin my walk home.

Two months later

I receive a voice note from an unsaved number: "We've been trying to call you several times now, but no one answers. We just wanted to know if you're OK and doing alright!" This turns out to be Tony, Tina's husband. They tell me their kids have asked about me, that they miss me, and that they'd like to invite me to their home for lunch. Listening to Tony's message ushers in a combination of exhilaration and relief I had thought no longer conceivable. I'm aware that healing knows no shortcuts, but realizing that, even in our Golgotha, we can, as Tina did, still choose to not entirely let go—to feel able to struggle, to survive—is crucial to recovery.

Later, in another Uber on my way to the couple's home, I am overwhelmed by a sense of peace and gratitude, even as Golgotha and its cloying memories remain raw. I realize that we can feel determined to struggle and to survive, that we must continue to connect in order to begin to heal. Perhaps, in time, and with our collective efforts, the more audible our pain, and our voices become, the more the silence, slow to thaw for so long, is replaced by our testimonies. These words, our right to write an existence not devoid of dignity, are what may keep us alive.

Afterword

In an Uber on the way to my gym, I pray there is no traffic. The driver talks about politics and our Golgotha, as the memories remain raw. I indicate where I was when it happened, that I was also in a taxi on my way to the gym.

"You were here, this close to the port? Were you with Jihad?"

I am unsure of his name.

"He has a gray Toyota Corolla."

He called him immediately. Having no way to reach out to each other when the debris began to lift, we are both relieved that the other had made it out. I ask what happened to his car. Having no other source of income, Jihad had somehow managed to gather the twenty million lira necessary to resurrect it and has since continued to drive for Uber.

Written by Sleiman El Hajj
Story contributed by Yvona Nehme

II. ON STRENGTH

The Fundamentals of Fire

T he fundamental expression of fire is action, or change. Fire enlivens my burning desire to keep moving forward in my growth, my knowledge, my deepening of yoga practices, and my enthusiasm for sharing it with others. Fire burns my ego and helps me get rid of patterns that no longer serve me. Fire reminds me of the important karmic imprint left from harming someone. Fire provides me with the energy I need to change myself and inspire others. Most of all, fire teaches me how to be in touch with that untamable element, harness its power and play with it, without ever burning to the ground.

On doomsday Tuesday, a 6 PM business meeting was scheduled to take place at my apartment in Gemmayze with a couple of my dearest friends, Rony and Lana. Lana sent me a message at around 5:30, saying she was running late and could not make it before 6:30. In my haste to finish some piled-up work, I failed to notify Rony about the time change, an omission that would result in a simmering guilt I'd carry for weeks around my neck, like a dead albatross. Rony, true to his nature, rang my doorbell at 6 PM. Sharp.

I love my home. I spend hours gazing out my beautifully carved windows. They don't make them like this anymore. Rounded vintage wooden frames that carry thin glass, embossed with complex arabesque that recall the nostalgia of a thriving '60s Beirut. This is also where I film my yoga practices that I use for my online guided sessions. The relationship I have with my home is sacred. As an architect, I've spent years working out the details. The entire apartment is covered with sculptures, artwork, and sentimental crystals and rocks that I have gathered over the years. This is my sanctuary, away from Beirut's noise, dust, and grime. Surrounded by tall and protective trees, stepping out onto my terrace often feels like I've gone for a walk in a lush Nordic wood.

I pour Rony a glass of water, and we instinctively move out. Beirut is hot this time of the year, and we are both grateful for the fresh air that gently blows in from the sea. Without needing an invitation, Rony stretches out on my wooden bench and smiles up at me.

I find our city, piled high in glass and concrete, to be oppressive and claustrophobic. But here on my terrace, here, dreams are made possible. Here, the air is invigorating, and the sky limitless. Here, I observe neighbors drinking coffee on balconies, one cigarette after the other. The quiet gossip and laments released from lips of the haggard and the young. Here, Rony and I plot and plan ways to elevate human consciousness through meditation, conscious breathing, and yoga. Here, we pour deep into the nature of the universe, fueled by a desire to make this world a better place. Here, all of Beirut is visible to me; the parts I love, and the parts I wish to improve upon. Here, all darkness is made visible, and on a clear day I can even see the ships coming into port.

In every chipped corner, every crumbling pillar, every light that goes dim, lessons waiting to be learned are everywhere to be found in the foundations of our daily lives. This much I keep learning, and more. The only way out of something is through it. Not away or around, not under or over, just in. Wherever we are on our evolutionary trajectory and however unsettling or frightening that position may be, the constant truth is that we are always in transition. From one minute to the other, from one breath to the next, paving the way towards the great unknown ...

My fingers trail along the gray metal balustrade and my mind jumps between our delayed meeting and this wonderful half hour of free time that suddenly presented itself to us. I am grateful for this stolen moment to sit with my best friend, my thought partner, my spirit brother. Over our years of work together, Rony and I have come to realize that not only are we colleagues but spiritual soul mates who perhaps have found each other, over and over again, across lifetimes. I observe a twinkle in his eyes, the excitement he never fails to hide upon the prospect of starting a new project. The gentle wrinkles and folds in his face, deeply set in stories of grand adventures from trekking the Himalayas to our adventures in the deep jungles of South America. What a blessing this friendship is in my life.

The first blast goes off.

Growing up between Lebanon and New York City, I witnessed war, suffering, and violence at a very young age. I fled to safer places a multitude of times throughout the interminable years of the Lebanese war. I was living in New York City when 9/11 changed our reality and worldwide history with it. Upon returning to Lebanon in 2005, I became part of the initial movement that took to the streets, reclaiming Lebanon from its remaining invaders. At Ground Zero on 9/11, I turned within and found a great strength that guided, supported, and kept me safe. It did the same at Martyrs' Square in Beirut in 2005 and in Gemmayze in 2020.

We jump from our seats to observe gray smoke moving very rapidly towards us. A sinister feeling sweeps through my stomach. My intuitive feeling is that the smoke is ushering in something far worse. I grab Rony by his shirt, urging him to go inside. I turn around and head in the direction of my living room, convinced he is right behind me. He isn't.

In my classes, I often encourage students to absorb the mechanics of transitions by focusing on the space between the yoga postures. Instead of methodically attending to the next pose, I challenge them to fully experience the moments that lead up to the actual position. The direction of their gaze, sweat emerging from skin pores, the breath, and most important, the pause in between breaths ... the delicate balance between movement and stillness. These precious moments in between are commonly known as "the journey."

Rony is on his journey. He lingers outside, pausing to observe and note the movement of smoke. And then, an ear-splitting crack and the second wave hits.

There is an entire distortion of time that until today is difficult to describe. I can't remember if the sound comes first or the wave. It is as if everything is happening simultaneously. Next thing I know, I am being projected by a force, an intensity, I have never experienced before. As I fly across the room, propelled by a wave of sound and pressure, there is a moment where everything seems to hang in the balance. It is not a thought or an intellectual musing. It is something else. A knowing. A deep understanding. Up there in midair, for a moment I catch a thought that proclaims, "I might die." But then, very quickly and before I land four meters back on the floor, a knowing takes over and assures me that I am going to be OK. Both thoughts are present: 50 percent death and 50 percent survival. But the strong knowing that I am going to be OK is the only thing that feels real, deep in my core.

August 4, 2020, is the longest transition from one breath to the next that I have ever taken in my life. I understand deep in my soul that all the work I have done in my life—twenty years of yoga and other spiritual practices, along with various therapy modalities—has prepared me for this day by raising my level of Awareness in my being. This ability to rest in pure Awareness, this is what is carrying me with grace this evening, and will during the days and months to come. Every moment in our lives—including the ones that are uncomfortable, painful, aggravating, and stressful—is a breath, and every breath could be our last, making every moment as precious as the next.

I lose consciousness for a few moments. My eyes are closed and I feel myself coming back to the sound of Rony's voice. He is calling my name. Rony—in his last-minute attempt to move inside—was also flung hard and rammed his head into a sharp object that remains unidentified to this day. I open my eyes and find him on his knees, holding his head in his hands, blood gushing from his forehead. The blast has hit him so hard that the carpet is now on top of him and a pool of blood underneath him. He slowly pushes himself up onto all fours. I crawl over to him, unaware of the level of destruction around me. I don't look around. All I see is blood. Rony's forehead is cracked open, and his right eye—which had brimmed with light and hope only moments ago—is dull and severely injured. Adrenaline kicks in, and bringing him to safety is all I can think about. As I run to the kitchen for some water to clean his wound and a towel to wrap around his head, I don't even realize that I'm also injured with cuts and bruises. I dash to to my bedroom and grab some cash, my passport, and my car keys, confident that we can make it to the emergency room in ten minutes. I realize I am in flip-flops, and an inner voice demands I change quickly into sneakers. Little do we know, a completely different reality is waiting for us outside.

Remaining anchored within oneself boils down to perspective. You can view life in terms of how much it churns you, cooks you, chews you, and then spits you out. Or you can view it in how much it nourishes you, waters you, shapes you, sustains you, glorifies you, celebrates you. We come to see that without the trials and tribulations inflicted by trouble, we would never recognize or fully appreciate the joy of simple pleasures.

The streets are covered with broken glass and rubble everywhere, making it impossible to take my car, or any car for that matter. Walking seems to be the best and quickest way to get help. We traverse the road and methodically make our way towards the Warde Hospital a few blocks away, just off Gemmayze's main street. Every single building along the way has been hit. People are sprawled out on the streets; some are hanging out of their windows screaming for help. A haggard man drenched in blood walks beside us, stumbling in confusion. We stop in our tracks. The hospital is demolished, along with the Red Cross center right next to it. Massive chunks of the buildings have been blown away. Windows shattered, walls crushed. People are staggering through what remains, drenched in blood. We are obviously dealing with something huge. I have to find another hospital.

The towel I have wrapped around Rony's head is now completely bright red. We have to move fast. Walking on Charles Malek Boulevard towards the Saint George Hospital, I pull out my phone and start making calls. Every person I'm able to reach has a similar story; they are either injured themselves or trying to help loved ones. The shattered glass prevents us all from getting to each other. There is no way we can make this on our own. Rony is going to bleed to death.

And it's all my fault, a dark and incessant thought crawls up. *I should have called. I should have told him the meeting was postponed.*

73

Holding back the tears, I navigate through my emotions, pushing past fear and focusing on different strategies to help keep Rony from losing consciousness. Hundreds of people around us are in the same situation. Somehow, in that moment, I feel my heart swell up. Whatever the situation, we are all in this together. All of Lebanon, it seemed. Collectively, we could figure it out.

And then, a small miracle.

Out of the blue, a young man on a moped stops right in front of us. "Get on," he says. *Get on what?* There is no space on this pint-sized vehicle, but somehow the two of us manage to make it aboard. He weaves his way through traffic so swiftly that I'm convinced our protruding knees are about to be crushed by the oncoming cars, and I cling on to his torso for dear life. Suddenly COVID-19 ceases to exist. We're flying. Within a few minutes, we arrive at the second hospital and our guardian angel takes off for a new rescue.

Walking towards the emergency room, a nurse raises her hands to stop us and screams, "Don't get closer, don't even try! We have dead people, dead staff …We can't take anyone!"

Resigned, we slump down on the street. Rony is beginning to lose consciousness. I hold him tight and whisper close to his ear, "Rony, keep talking to me, say anything, and breathe, just breathe." We sit there on the concrete, in the eye of the storm, waiting for something to happen.

This is when the second miracle happens.

A young nun driving by stops after seeing us distressed. She tells us to jump in and promises to get us to another hospital towards Geitawi . We are stuck in dense traffic with so many people in a similar situation. The nun's phone rings. Her sister has been injured and she has to go get her. She apologizes profusely and we, of course, understand. Once again on the pavement, I know I have to get in touch with my core strength and get creative with my solutions.

Two hours have elapsed since we left home, and there is no sign of hope in sight. I close my eyes and clear my head. Years of meditation practice have helped me find my focus quicker and quicker over the years. And there it is. The answer presents itself in a flash.

I call my client Michel, a plastic surgeon. Maybe he can help.

And then the third miracle.

He picks up. He is on his way down from the mountains and asks me to try and get to his clinic, where he promises to meet us. Luckily it is only a five-minute walk. We arrive only to find that his building has also been destroyed. Making our way up the stairs, we climb over broken steel frames and concrete blocks. His assistant is already there, and the three of us look around the clinic in disbelief. There is nowhere to stand, let alone sit. She and I clear the operating table from debris, and Rony is finally able to lay down. After administering some painkillers, Michel arrives. I cringe thinking that Rony will have to be operated on without any anesthesia. I pray there is no infection. Michel immediately starts working on him. Rony holds my hand, squeezing it from the pain. After completing the stitches, Michel takes me by my shoulders and looks me straight in the eye. "Surgery is needed now," he says, with great compassion. "Otherwise, he *will* lose his eye."

It is time to connect back to pure focus. In these moments, time ceases to exist. Beirut ceases to exist. All that is present, is presence. Emptiness, nothingness, vastness… A feeling of "I am" and "I am nothing at all" fuses, and it is within this unison that I find the most silent and peaceful state of being I have ever experienced. I can't hear the screams, shattered glass, sirens, or wails. All I can feel is our breath, in unison, in union, working together.

We spend our lives in constant movement. Searching for answers in the external world. We travel, we seek, we yearn, we desire, we need, we grind, we hustle, we persevere in our mad pursuits of Truth. Yet all the answers lay within. So often, we are oblivious that all the answers are right there, sitting right at the center of our chest, pervading every cell of our being, simply waiting to be activated.

I hold Rony's hand, and my eyes trace the pulsating veins on his neck. For a moment, I feel gratitude. I feel so grateful to have an ocean of precious opportunities and teachings to touch upon, understand, and integrate into that moment. Life has me humbled. I gently wipe some blood from across Rony's face and give him a smile. We are going to figure this out. We will pass this exercise with grace. Perhaps it is not a coincidence that we are experiencing this day together.

And then, in perfect timing, the fourth miracle.

Rony's friend Hussein arrives to help. It is dark now and the three of us walk towards Rony's, where Hussein's car is parked, almost embodying the destruction around us. When we arrive at a blown-in door I run in, grab a change of clothes for him, and check on the rest of the house. Realizing anyone could walk in, I call our close friend Mark to see if he can come collect any valuables.

"I'm on it," he says, without hesitation.

Hussein secures an ophthalmologist in Saida, a half-hour drive away. For a second, I think about COVID-19. As if the explosion isn't enough, we are also enduring this vicious pandemic as well as hyperinflation that has collapsed the already corrupt and failed state. I scream as I climb into the car, only just realizing that I am also injured. I have been walking around for the past three hours with a big chunk of glass lodged into my lower back and small shards throughout my entire body. I fold over to avoid contact with the back seat and calm myself down through focused breathing as we take off. Rony jokingly asks if he should cancel his client appointments for tomorrow.

As they prep Rony for surgery, I am taken into a room. I strip down and instinctively throw my bloodied and punctured overalls in the trash. As the nurse cleans me up, I observe all the cuts and lesions across my body, astonished that I was that badly hurt. I want to rush back to Rony as soon as she has finished but I have no clothes. Luckily, Hussein has his gym bag in the car and soon supplies me with an oversized T-shirt and really big shorts that hang off my petite frame. I walk into Rony's room with Hussein and the three of us crack up. Laughter spurs tears of joy and relief.

We are safe, for now.

Epilogue

My story doesn't end here.

The night I got home from the hospital, I almost lost my father. He suffers from Alzheimer's, and in many ways I wondered if he was able to feel everything that happened. He had been quite stable, but that night his vitals suddenly began to drop. Things add up quite quickly in Lebanon. And these things can take a toll. We had to call in the paramedics, and I was now edging on forty-eight hours without sleep.

That night, the fifth and final miracle happened.

My father, who had been lost in the cruel world of this disease for quite a few years now, found his way back to me for just a few seconds. We locked eyes and smiled in recognition.

Everything is going to be OK, his soul reassured me. I held his hand and reassured him back. *I know Dad, somehow I know.*

My father decided he was finally ready to leave his body a few months later.

I strongly believe he stuck around long enough to make sure that I was OK.

Grief and loss make it hard at first to accept the parts of ourselves that have been forever changed, but when I choose to feel so that I can heal, softness sets in, and the paradigm starts to shift. Grief has allowed me to discover the new me that is percolating under the surface of my turbulent emotional landscape. Whatever it is I am feeling, there is a place for all of it. Grief has allowed me to show up in the skin of my most authentic, compassionate self and be witnessed in all my vulnerability. Grief has carved in me an opening to more love and gratitude, deeper self-knowledge, a broader vision, greater possibilities, and the promise of a newfound purpose. Grief, the great initiator of change, has never failed to teach me that out of the darkest pain comes the deepest wisdom.

Have I healed? To be honest, I can't say that I have fully arrived at this hopeful conclusion. Almost a year on, what the news and media always fail to cover is the aftermath of such a catastrophic event, how shock and trauma come to afflict an entire nation, affecting our daily lives in the long term. Rony's eye is still sewn shut, and it is likely that he will never regain the sight in it. Because of COVID-19 restrictions, he is unable to fly abroad for specialized surgery.

So the truth is, I don't want to be hopeful just yet, not as long as justice has not been served. There can be no healing without justice, there just can't. None of us has fully recovered. Perhaps, we never will. And perhaps, it is still too soon to even consider.

What happened shattered my core, but I am working hard on allowing the deep hope to come through. Perhaps hope paves the way for justice in the end.

The energy of fire, if not used cautiously, can and will burn one to the ground, but fire, if used wisely, can also result in purification, transformation, and renewal.

Written by Zena el Khalil
Contributed by Danielle Abisaab

All italicized writing originally appeared on Danielle's Instagram page, @yoga_holic. Knowing Danielle to be a gifted writer, the author wanted to share Danielle's actual words and teachings where possible.

The Pledge

I solemnly pledge myself before God and in the presence of this assembly, to pass my life in purity and to practice my profession faithfully. I will abstain from whatever is deleterious and mischievous, and will not take or knowingly administer any harmful drug. I will do all in my power to maintain and elevate the standard of my profession, and will hold in confidence all personal matters committed to my keeping, and all family affairs coming to my knowledge in the practice of my calling. With loyalty will I endeavor to aid the physician in his work, and as a "missioner of health" I will dedicate myself to devoted service to human welfare.

—The Florence Nightingale Pledge

I t was a Tuesday, the first in that month of August. The sun was set to fade at seven-thirty in the Greater Beirut area.

In the soft haze of summertime, twenty-six-year-old Pamela Zeinoun was preparing to end her shift in the neonatal unit of Saint George Hospital, about two kilometers away from the Port of Beirut.

The mother of two babies in her care had left the hospital at around 4:30 PM. In the crux of the cataclysmic hour, she, along with her husband and brother, was at home with the third triplet.

At 6 PM, after having spent the day bathing the babies in her ward, playing with them, and keeping them warm for their parents' imminent return, Pamela was updating the system before wrapping up her workday.

"Hi, Mama," she said to her own mother on the phone, "*Yalla, ana* almost *khallaset!* I need about an hour and I'll be home… *Senye* mama, one sec, there's a very strange smell. *Yi!*"

At that exact moment, as the cruel irony of time would have it, a devastating boom shook the world around and within her. "Oh my God, mama, *shou hay?! What was that!* Ma-"

Everything went dark. Calamity ensued.

A few neighborhoods away, the ground underneath the triplets' family also quaked in violent rage.

"*Shou sar!? Shou sar!*" the mother's quavering voice cried to her husband.

"What in the name of God just happened?" As the doors and windows of their home shuddered fiercely, all this mother of three could think about was whether her two premature newborns had made it out alive from whatever just happened.

Within seconds, news of the shattering of the heart of Beirut was everywhere. BREAKING NEWS: EXPLOSION IN BEIRUT. JUST IN: NUMBER OF CASUALTIES ON THE RISE. JUST IN: EXPLOSION IN LEBANON. انفجير. انفـجـار. انفـجـار. BEIRUT. PORT OF BEIRUT. انفجـار.

سقوط إصابات
injuries

ضحايا
casualties

ضحايا
victims

victims

ضحايا
victims

ضحايا

In Pamela's ruptured world, everything had gone dark, exploded, and shattered as the horrible smell of chemicals permeated the wreckage surrounding her. Dust and destruction were everywhere. Stuck under heavy piles of false ceiling, she had no idea what just happened. In a matter of seconds, she had been thrown across the room and covered in everything—glass, ceiling, stone, dust, weight, weight, weight.

At first, Pamela mistook it for a terrorist attack, believing that a consecutive explosion was on the way. For a second she thought, *This is it,* and that it would be best not to move and spend her final moments on earth in labored tranquility.

It's done. I'm either dead, or will die in a second. She closed her eyes in surrender.

After a few seconds of muffled inertia, the nurses' oath came to her, overpowering her with an urge: *I solemnly pledge myself before God and in the presence of this assembly, to pass my life in purity and to practice my profession faithfully.* She thought of her parents, and how just footsteps away there were five newborns who couldn't breathe on their own. She thought of how precious their lives were for their parents. Each moment they get to hold them, each gram of weight they grow into.

Pamela began to bring her body back into reality, reminding herself that it is neither the moment to panic nor to cry. She did not know the extent of the injury she may have sustained. *Since I'm able to open my eyes, perhaps I can move my hand,* and she did. Then she tried to move her legs. Despite all the weight upon her, she was able, with bloodied hands cut by splinters of glass, to push herself up for the sake of the tiny bodies in her care.

All the plexiglass incubators sheltering the babies were smashed. She approached them, removing the debris and wreckage on top, working with utmost speed in fear of another possible explosion, her eyes constantly searching for the lack of red.

Since she could not open the incubators, she had to pull the newborns out through their separate windows with the help of a colleague. Wearing nothing but diapers, the babies would die of cold if she did not keep them as warm as possible. Pamela cradled the fragile bodies of three babies, the two siblings and a third, while a fellow nurse carried the remaining two newborns. Bearing the many risks in mind, they clawed their way out in the utter darkness, through corridors blocked by ruptured doors, in a desperate attempt to keep them alive.

"I'm sorry," she kept saying to their tucked heads. "I'm so sorry!"

For the next two hours, the fate of their precious babies was a fading mirage for their parents. The view onto the Port of Beirut from her hospital room window haunted the mother of the triplets. She, along with her husband and brother, desperately tried to reach the neonatal unit, first through the cut telephone lines and then immediately with their own dumbstruck bodies, rushing into the heart of the pandemonium.

So much debris was strewn across the streets to the ground floor of the hospital that they could barely cross over. The doors, the ceilings, the lights—everything was gone. Everything was destroyed. She could not shake off the unbearable thought of having lost a child.

Her husband and brother ran up to the neonatal unit, each step forward as heavy as the anticipation. They were unprepared for the sight they were about to behold. They were in this building only a few hours ago, yet nothing was the same. Nothing. The hospital was in absolute ruins. Despite there being so much tragic uproar enveloping them, the world seemed ominously silent.

They pushed through the crushed walls and remains of the ceiling of the unit. They caught sight of the smashed incubators under the rubble. Breathless, in cold sweat, they approached what would have been the most horrendous thing they would have to ever see. But the incubators were empty, except for the babies' pacifiers. Not even a drop of blood. The two men looked at each, completely disoriented, until one finally broke the silence:

"*Wen henne?!* Where are they?!"

In Pamela's trembling arms, the three babies, with a collective weight of no more than ten pounds, were held tight, unaware of the dangers of the world they came into earlier than expected. While descending the dilapidated stairs, she felt one baby slipping from her. She held him up and squeezed them all as close as she could. Even though she held three small bodies in her arms, she was not aware of their actual state. Were they truly OK? Were they conscious? In deep sleep? She was cradling them and they were not crying, but that was all she knew. She pushed through the darkened halls, through the havoc, looking for a possible evacuation exit. All the while she prayed to God to give her the strength to keep her legs strong so she could reach the ground floor, where she could check up on the babies' condition.

She finally reached the ground floor, where she was shocked to encounter nurses, doctors, residents, patients holding their IVs—all screaming, shouting, and blood-soaked. The medical staff were struggling to help as many of the wounded as possible. People were flocking into the hospital for help while the staff was undergoing an emergency evacuation. The staff, the same people she had smiled "good afternoon" to only a few hours ago. No one knew what had happened. No one knew what was going to happen.

The Saint George urgent care unit had collapsed, and there was no chance of receiving any help. Pamela had risked the babies' lives by taking them out of their incubators, but she had no other choice. She had promised to take care of them. She had pledged an oath to do so.

She looked around at the encompassing turmoil and then into the babies' faces. They were so innocent and fragile. She knew what she needed to do. She made sure their skins were still pink, that their small bodies were still warm, and headed out.

Everything outside was dust-gray. The color red stained every human in cruel juxtaposition. Heaps of people crowded the hospital doors.

"*Allah yse'dik*!" people told her. "May God help you!" they cried, their faces full of hopeless terror. Strangers approached Pamela asking how they could help. "Please, *'toune tyeb. Shi. Hayalla shi la ghattiyon*! Please give me clothes, anything, to cover them up," she pleaded. "Please *khede hay*," a security guard took off his shirt and handed it to her. "Please take this so I will have offered you all the help I am able to offer."

Pamela walked for kilometers with each child wrapped in the clothes of another. Her phone was in her pocket the entire time, ringing continuously, but she had no hands to answer. Her hands were only there to hold. That was all she cared about. She couldn't feel her arms. They were numb. But she wasn't only carrying the babies, she was also carrying the parents of both families. They were all her responsibility. She knew her parents must have been terrified, but they would eventually know she was OK.

While searching for another nearby hospital, she came across unfathomable, endless destruction. Balconies were falling. Buildings were cracking. She could hear herself walking over splinters of shattered glass. People filled the streets, running, crying, panicking. No one had any idea what was happening. She would occasionally hear people say there was going to be another strike, another explosion. It was very possible that this would happen, and they would all perish together. Cars were clumped in gridlock traffic, held back by the loud upheaval of horns, sirens, and cries for help. On impulse, she got into one car, moved for a few seconds, and then got back out, realizing the babies needed warmth and could not handle inactivity. There was no time to lose. It was a matter of life and death. Pamela kept on walking.

At first, Pamela had assumed that only Saint George had been wiped out by the blast, but she and her babies were turned away at the first hospital, and the second—both devastated. To reach a third, it took Pamela ninety minutes on foot, five kilometers through rubble, glass, and utter havoc, with three premature newborns in her arms. Even when her every vein was stinging with hopelessness, Pamela made sure all three heads were facing her chest, as it was inconceivable for her to let them see the surrounding horror.

The hospital in Jal El Dib, a completely different governorate, was swamped with the bleeding and injured. Pamela implored a nun on the nursing staff for an incubator: "*Ma soeur*, Please, *se'dine*! *'ayze* incubator! *Daroure*! Please! *Law bas wehde*! Just one, sister! Please," she begged.

"*Fi 'anna bas wehde. Shoufe shou fike ta'mle.*" The sister told her they only had one.

After nearly two hours of roaming frenzied streets in search of a machine to bathe the babies in life-giving oxygen, Pamela's shivering hands finally placed the twins and the jaundiced baby into an incubator. They settled in, all wrapped up in tranquil sleep, completely unaware of the chaos around them. Pamela was still soaked in shock and disquietude. She called her colleagues to tell them where she was, and asked them to relay a message to the parents.

"They need not worry. Ali, Noah, and Cedra are all s-s-s-safe. They're with me. They're s-s-s-safe," she said, unable to control the shaking.

Her colleague found the mother of triplets collapsed on the floor of the neonatal unit, staring at the ceiling, begging to see her newborns. When they finally arrived at the hospital, the mothers of the children were in absolute emotional despair. One even grabbed Pamela's hands, begging to see her babies. When Pamela saw the parents reunited with their children, all the horror she had witnessed evaporated, and the jitters in her bones settled to an undertone.

Pamela could not sleep for two days afterward. How could she risk shutting her eyes after witnessing so much? How could anyone in Beirut go to sleep with absolutely no guarantee of waking up to another disaster? Following the tragedy, she lost about ten kilograms. The entire staff of Saint George Hospital were provided with psychological consultation. As for Pamela, telling her story, and the cascade of public gratitude, provided greatly needed comfort, though she continues to insist that every nurse was a hero that day, every single one.

Like thousands of people who were close to the Beirut port that day, Pamela's survival was a roll of the dice. Hundreds lost the vicious gamble they had no idea was being wagered. Thousands of others who may have been physically spared have lost all spark for life. For Pamela, death no longer has anything to do with the somatic. Death has claimed its corner in her every waking day.

In the little Middle Eastern once-upon-a-time gem called Lebanon, August 4 will never be a clear day. In the remaining parts of the world, the 4th of August is National Chocolate Chip Cookie Day. It is also Single Working Women's Day, National White Wine Day, and the day Louis Armstrong was born—his birth carrying the seed of "What a Wonderful World."

Written by Perla Kantarjian
Story contributed by Pamela Zeinoun

With Grit and Grace

In the summer of 1993, Meriam, a wide-eyed, afraid eighteen-year-old Filipina steps onto the tarmac of Beirut International Airport. Fueled with excitement and anxiety, she meets a grumpy, hairy twenty-something Lebanese male, Ali. He speeds up the airport process and ushers her and a dozen other girls into his minivan to drop each one off at her new home.

Ali turns up the radio as he swerves through the streets of this strange and intriguing city. With each bump the car dances, swaying the girls on the bus along to the beat. Meriam soaks the city in. Her fellow passengers don't share the same enthusiasm. They keep to themselves until their name is called. As they walk up the aisle to leave the bus, they're met with uneasy smiles of encouragement from their sisters.

After thirty minutes it is finally Meriam's turn. The van pulls up to an older building down a minuscule street in Mar Elias. Ali rushes Meriam out, "*Yalla, Yalla khalseeneh! Ma fee mahal suf!*" He sticks his head out of the window to yell at some people behind. "Wlo sennye! Shu khas deena la immeh?!" Confused,

87

Meriam smiles at him blankly. He barks at her, *"Yalla go zer iz* your madame."

A rush of positivity floods her body as she leaves the van. She reassures herself by repeating the fairytale stories she heard in Manila. *They will be my new family. They will give me a home. I will make good money for my parents.*

Meriam's madame is impatiently waiting at the building's doorstep. "Hi, mada—" Meriam's bright smile is met with indifference. "Where your passport? Give me now!" Suddenly the sirens and honks from the jammed street burst Meriam's bubble of positivity. Her stomach flips. Her madame looks deranged.

Her gut instinct doesn't fail her. She repeatedly endures hair pulling, hitting, and verbal abuse. One night her madame's craziness peaks to unprecedented levels. After a beating that leaves her on the ground in a puddle of her own urine, she decides enough is enough. So, in the middle of the night, she musters up the courage to escape. This traumatizing event awakens the grit that resides within Meriam. This is her power and it will rescue her multiple times over.

Now a widowed mother of two, Meriam returns to Beirut in 2010. This time, she lands in a renovated Beirut Rafik Hariri International Airport. The process is a bit different. Madame is the one who picks you up. It's rainy and cold. Meriam drags her luggage and looks for her madame. She finds her holding up a sign.

Meriam is now wiser and cautious. She studies her madame intensely. Meriam is rushed to the car where four kids are arguing over a bag of chips. As they drive off, madame starts to speak loudly over her screaming children, laying down the law: "No mobile phone. No days off."

Anxiety suffuses Meriam's body like a recurring bad dream. She frantically searches for any way to wake herself up. At a stoplight, she musters the courage to open the door and run. Now Meriam roams the streets of Beirut with only the clothes on her back.

The weight of her obligations at home fills her with shame and the fear of disappointing not only her father and mother but her kids too. Meriam knows she can't go back home. Her two sons are depending on her.

Technically a fugitive, Meriam tricks the system. Without a single document in hand, she has to find an employer willing to take on the risk of hiring an undocumented worker. So she keeps her eyes open. She's ready to take anything she can get. This time her purpose runs deeper than her own personal survival.

Every penny is for her sons. She has to provide.

Connected by fragmented words and whispers, the migrant community majestically comes together. Regardless of nationality, predicament, or background, migrant workers give each other tips to help survive the unforgiving and harsh realities they face daily in Lebanon. Through this grapevine, she hears of a job that asks no questions but demands long hours. Meriam gratefully takes it despite the fourteen-, sometimes sixteen-hour shifts.

Day in, day out, she follows the same ritual, like a film on repeat, waking up early, putting on a housemaid uniform, and heading out. She keeps her gaze low, avoiding authorities at all costs. A few bus rides later she arrives at the hotel, where she changes out of the housemaid uniform and into that of the hotel. The uniform is a simple decoy she cunningly wears to avoid being asked for papers. The very thing she ran away from is her coat of armor.

She doesn't take any days off. When the hotel insists on it, she finds an odd job to fill her time. Every dollar is calculated and saved. Meriam has a purpose. She is avoiding the shame of running away from her legal job and the guilt of being so far away from her babies. And although these are three of the loneliest years of her life, she is sure the distance and sacrifice will be worth it.

Hardened by routine, Meriam's skin becomes thicker and her eye wiser, so it is only natural that she is skeptical when she first meets her next employers. For the first couple of months, she is hesitant. She fears that letting down her guard will reveal their bad side. But it becomes rapidly apparent that these are good people. They truly care about her well-being, her impact on the world, her story.

They repeatedly encourage Meriam to use her voice and join the activist migrant worker community. She attends meetings over the weekends and is astonished. *How are they so courageous? Aren't they scared of deportation? Imprisonment?* She silently listens and observes until she finally finds the courage to share her own story. By the time she finishes, every woman in the circle is in tears.

At thirty-seven, Meriam finds her voice. She becomes the brave migrant activist Lebanon desperately needs. The grit that resides within her finally finds a space to express itself. She finds her calling. She joins several NGOS and runs protests, roundtables, and conferences, all in the name of helping domestic migrant workers gain their rights.

A few years later, when the time comes for the family to leave Lebanon, their relationship with Meriam isn't that of mere employer and employee. She is family. And so, as family, they insist on continuing to pay for her visa, so she'll never have to be at anyone's mercy ever again. The papers give her validity, and somehow they make her feel like a free woman. Meriam is legal, and there is absolutely nothing stopping her. She has found her voice and her light. She has learned to unapologetically be herself.

In 2015, Meriam becomes a day nanny for an expat family with newborn twin girls. She shows up at the house early in the morning and leaves in the evening. Although her days are fourteen hours long, the job allows her to continue working with the community. She has her autonomy.

In the summer of 2020, as the world goes into lockdown, her employers and her roommate get stuck in their home countries. Meriam is also stuck—alone in her Mar Mikhael home. She is meant to be back home with her sons, but like the rest of the world, she is frozen in time. She can't help but wallow. The silence is getting to her. It is tough for her to be still and do nothing; it reminds her of her loneliness. So, Meriam being Meriam, she channels her energy into something positive and finds purpose.

With the impending financial and health crisis, Meriam can't help but think of the domestic workers stranded across remote villages in Lebanon. These women are trapped in homes no longer able to provide salaries and, in some cases, food. She has to find a way to fight for these vulnerable women. She organizes online workshops and conferences with the migrant community to put together a plan. Along with a few other ladies, she travels across Lebanon in buses to provide in-need domestic workers with aid and relief kits.

By early July, the world starts to open up again. Finally, after months of postponing, Meriam receives word that her employers are scheduled to return to Beirut. She is filled with joy. This means life is going back to normal. She misses the warmth of the family, of their old Beirut home filled with grandeur and history. But mostly she misses the twins. Their bright smiles and little giggles fill her heart with joy. She realizes just how much she depends on them with them gone.

In the meantime, things are not as normal as she'd hoped for. Her employers are unnerved by COVID-19 and on edge about the ongoing financial crisis. They ask her to slow down on her aid trips and restrict the number of places she visits and people she meets with. She reluctantly complies because, although her humanitarian instincts run strong, her love for the twins is even stronger.

Tuesday is a big day. After three months, Meriam's roommate and best friend is finally returning. She promises to come home early and cook a welcome-back dinner. It feels great to have a social life again, someone to let off some steam and discuss the last couple of months with. She asks to leave work slightly earlier than the usual so she can pass by the grocer for ingredients.

Meriam finishes washing the dishes in the old kitchen sink, which has faucets with ridges like most old Lebanese homes. The girls are running between her legs, chanting, "Manga stay! Manga stay!" When they were young, Meriam was a little hard to pronounce, so they came up with the nickname Manga and it stuck.

As she slings on her purse and heads to the door, she negotiates, "I have to go now, but I promise tomorrow morning I'll be here early, and you know what? I'll make any breakfast you want!"

A large dark cloud in the distance next to Burj Al Ghazzal catches Meriam's eye. At first, she thinks it's a thunderstorm, which is very unusual in the sticky month of August. The twins' father, who is pacing back and forth on a work call, also sees it. They both stop at the window and stare for a minute. It's not a storm. This ominous dark black cloud has a distinct shape and color. It isn't natural.

Suddenly they hear an explosion. The loud sound fills every inch of Meriam's body. She feels it in her bones, in her face, in her cheeks. Everything vibrates. Her body sways. The girls burst into tears.

Meriam's motherly instincts kick in. She scoops up the children and runs from the window and into the hallway. Their mother comes out of her study, and, with the father, they follow her.

Then the earth shakes. Doorways burst out of place. Cabinets and glass explode. The girls are wailing, their parents silent and pale. The ringing is so loud that Meriam doesn't know if she is hearing sirens or if it is all in her imagination. All she knows for sure is that they need to get out of the old building or else it might collapse. She frantically runs down the stairs with the girls firmly in her grip. Their parents follow without thinking.

Truth be told, she doesn't know what to do, but her gut instinct drives her all the way to St. Joseph. She feels like the week-old renovated church could be some kind of refuge from whatever war was going on. As they run over, Meriam doesn't think to look at or help anyone. She has to get the girls to safety. They only realize the church has also been affected when they arrive. The parents try to make calls, but the lines are down.

People come together, as people do in times of crisis. Rumors about what caused this explosion flood the parking lot. They learn it came from the port, but no one knows whether or not it was an act of war.

The lines finally started working again and a friend gets through to Meriam's employers. They decide to take refuge in a mountain house. Meriam offers to go back to their now crumbling home to gather things for the girls, so they'd have some sort of comfort. On her way she notices just how much blood is on the floor. So much blood. *Where is it coming from?*

In the rush of it all, she realizes she's forgotten to check on her sister in Ain el-Mreisseh. She keeps calling but there is no answer. She finally gets through and is reassured that they are fine and the damage is minimal, just some broken glass.

She reaches the entrance to the beautiful Beirut building, and as she starts going up the stairs, she realizes she doesn't have the keys.

How am I going to get in? For a brief second, she forgets what happened, forgets the state they left the house in. She finds the door in pieces on the landing, as if a bulldozer rammed through the windows, purposefully trying to tear down the heritage home. The building is collapsing. Pieces of the roof are making a loud sound as they fall to the ground. Meriam trembles as she packs. She runs back to the family, hands them the luggage, gives the girls their favorite teddies, and kisses them goodbye. A part of her wonders if this is the last time she'll ever see them. She wishes them good luck and tells them to reach out once they settle.

She makes her way to her home to Mar Mikhael through the back streets of Achrafieh and begins to take in the damage of all the beautiful buildings. Her heart falls to the ground.

What about my old apartment building? What about my roommate?

Meriam is frantic. The entire street is a mess, a post-apocalyptic scene. The smell of gasoline sharply cuts through the atmosphere. Trees, signs, and flowers are strewn about. Cars are frozen in the middle of the road, some facing the wrong direction. People are running aimlessly. Some are wailing, others are in shock. Blood is everywhere, glistening on a sea of glass.

The sun is setting and there are no streetlights. Meriam walks slowly, cautiously, like in a minefield, watching her every step. Every minute feels like a year. Her ears keep ringing.

Led by the soft glow of her mobile phone, Meriam arrives to find her roommate sitting in the living area crying in absolute shock. Meriam goes to her and wraps her up in a long, tight embrace. "We're OK, *hamdillah*. We will be OK, I promise. Our home is OK."

After some moments of rest, Meriam runs into her room to open the safe in the back of her closet. Her most prized possession is still there. Not the hard-earned money she has gathered over the years or her memory box, but her papers. Her freedom.

Surviving the explosion shifts something in Meriam's core. In Lebanon's brokenness she finds a purpose. In a country that was always temporary, in a chapter almost at its end, she chooses her home.

Written by Tala Arakji
Story contributed by Meriam Prado

The Night Calls

Note: Pseudonyms have been used throughout this story.

I lost my country

"I lost my country. I am suffocating. I need to talk to someone. I need to pay my condolences to my country. Can I pay my condolences to you?"

Nadim texted a mental health support line in Beirut a few nights after the port explosion destroyed swathes of the capital. He needed to talk to someone and, as a Lebanese expatriate living in Australia, none around him could understand how he felt.

"Please, don't think I lost anyone in the explosion. I just lost my country."

At the receiving end of Nadim's messages was Maryam, who had opened a mental health support line with her friend Rayan the morning after the explosion. She had limited training, but knew she could answer Nadim and the hundreds more that would end up texting her.

August 4

Maryam was working from her home in the green mountain town of Achqout, far from Beirut. The company she worked with had recently relocated to brand-new offices in Mar Mikhael. They had moved their desks and supplies to start working on location in September. She was on a call with two people when they suddenly dropped out. She thought she heard one of them say something abruptly, right before the screen went black, but she didn't quite catch it. Not a moment later, Maryam's partner sent her a short message:

"I love you."

This was odd. They usually didn't send each other such messages in the middle of a workday. Her mom stormed into her room. A door had slammed out of nowhere and she wanted to know if Maryam had felt the earthquake as well, but she hadn't. Maryam received another message from a friend: "Explosion in Beirut."

Her heart stopped. Her partner's message had a whole other meaning.

Maryam suddenly felt really cold, freezing even, dread spreading from her fingers and feet through the rest of her body.

Was it an attack? Things were tense with Israeli drones constantly flying over the country. *A targeted assassination? Where did it happen? How big was it?* Nothing really made sense.

The first image and then another. The videos, the screams and cries, sirens, sounds of broken glass and panic. The frantic messages sent to jamming networks, checking up on loved ones:

"Where's Maria? She's not responding."

"My mom is down there and she's not picking up!"

"Please tell me you're home and not in Beirut!!"

"I'm OK, just material damage."

"House was hit but I'm OK."

"I'm OK."

The pink cloud was everywhere.

As the injured poured into hospitals, people began to realize the extent of the catastrophe and Maryam started receiving different kinds of messages:

"Blood needed."

The requests were for relatives of friends at first, but she soon started receiving urgent demands for blood units across the city. With years of experience in community engagement and organizing, Maryam focused on what she could do and created a group blood drive on WhatsApp, directing people to specific centers and hospitals. Requests were fulfilled in minutes, with people even driving down from the mountains to donate their blood to Beirut.

There is hope, Maryam thought.

The next morning

Maryam couldn't sleep. Her mind wouldn't let her. At 3 AM she received a request for blood for a boy in critical condition. She wasn't sure why the call came in so late, considering hospitals had stopped requests two hours earlier. *Maybe he was found under the rubble late or his health deteriorated fast?* She couldn't do much. Everyone she knew who could donate had already done so. A ding woke her up at 5 AM. The boy had received the blood he needed.

Maryam hadn't realized she fell asleep until she woke up again at seven. She couldn't place how she was feeling, so she focused on completing tasks. She paced back and forth between the living room and her bedroom, making a list of what needed to get done: Help relocate people who lost their homes. Get food, water, medical supplies, all kinds of cleaning supplies. *If I get extra brooms and gloves, I can get other people to help.* She had a nagging feeling that there was more to be done. She called her friend Rayan.

"How are you feeling?" he asked.

This wasn't an easy question to answer. Maryam knew that even though she was far from Beirut, even though she and her loved ones were all physically safe, she really needed support that morning. She began to identify her feelings while talking to Rayan: numb, anxious, panicked, scared, guilty, nervous, restless, helpless. Hopeless. *But I'm not a victim. If I feel this way, what about those who lost their homes? Or their loved one? What about people who were injured? Or those who tended to the injured? What about the parents who lived through the civil war and now had to reassure their traumatized children? What about people like me?*

The next step was clear. Maryam and Rayan set up a support line using their own private numbers. Rayan knew one mental health professional, and by 11 AM, they had three therapists on standby. By 1 PM, they were six. Two hours later, they were sharing an announcement on social media.

The system was simple and straightforward. Rayan and Maryam would receive the calls and forward all caller information to the therapists, who would immediately follow up. Armed with the items on her list, Maryam went to Mar Mikhael to do something. She needed to do something. She had to receive the first call in Beirut.

Chaos and glass

As she walked down the streets of Mar Mikhael, all Maryam could focus on was the sound of glass being swept, as if it were breaking over and over again. She could also hear men yelling instructions as they loaded rubble onto trucks, the voices of firefighters as they searched buildings for survivors, the security forces trying to clear out cars that had driven into the area. But mostly she heard glass. Crushing under her feet, amplifying her every step.

Numbness. She had to focus.

She saw Locale, the bar right next to Tante Siham's *dekkeneh*, known for the old dog that would sleep in front of it. Maryam and her friends loved spending summer evenings sitting at Locale's high tables on the sidewalk. They loved how anyone passing by had to walk in between them. They loved the music and the drinks, the conversation and the company. Locale was now just a pile of broken wood, glass, and debris, like the once-gas station across the street, like the building partly collapsed next door.

Dread.

She had to focus.

It seemed like everything that anyone had ever owned was strewn on the ground in front of her. There were shoes hanging from electricity wires, wooden window shutters on the sidewalk, and old red tiles of what must have been someone's roof.

She was the first to arrive at her partner's apartment, but Maryam walked right in. There was no front door left to open. Only one windowpane had survived, the one her partner had cracked open to let some air in, relieving the pressure from the explosion. She started shoveling, sweeping, cleaning, salvaging whatever she could.

Guilt.

She had to focus.

All the stories she heard and spaces she cleaned after his apartment mixed together in a hazy blur. She didn't have time to feel, to let emotion in.

She had to focus.

She was needed. People needed her. They would need the mental health support line.

The first call came in at 6 PM. The therapist who received the call texted the group immediately after: "We have to get this hotline out to more people."

It was too much

Sarah's teenage daughter hadn't spoken since the explosion, hiding in her silence, but when Sarah called the hotline, she tried her best to sound cheerful and crack jokes.

He was a member of the security forces who was ready to end his life, sitting with a loaded firearm. His call was his last attempt to reach out and find a reason to stay. He was exhausted, overwhelmed, helpless, unable to help his own people due to his position. He felt he was of no use for anyone. The therapist who helped him, who talked him out of suicide, could no longer continue with the hotline.

It was all too much.

People were trying to cope in the aftermath of the explosion and didn't know how to feel. Maryam was taking all the requests, and though she had no background in mental health, she knew she could facilitate the process. She studied. She read about how to deal with victims of trauma. She scrolled through mental health posts on social media. She set up a protocol: take the call, write down the caller's name and number, acknowledge their pain and reassure them, and inform them that a therapist would be contacting them soon. She made it clear that she was only a facilitator, not a mental health professional, and that one would be in contact shortly. Even though she tried to take on this responsibility as best she could, she couldn't help but feel with each and every one of the callers: numb, anxious, panicked, scared, guilty, nervous, restless, helpless. Hopeless.

It was all too much.

"My husband is no longer my husband. He is not eating. He is not talking. He is not doing anything. He is just sitting. What can I do? How can I talk to him? This is not my husband. I will lose him if I don't do anything."

Nancy called about one week after the explosion and refused to hang up or wait to have her request forwarded to a therapist. After a local radio station broadcast the details of the hotline and gave out Maryam's number every hour on the hour, her phone wouldn't stop ringing. She expected to be contacted mainly via text message and was surprised when people actually called. There was a sense of urgency. People needed help right away. People like Nancy.

So Maryam listened. She first tried to calm Nancy down, but when she was unsuccessful, she simply offered reassurance, telling her she was heard and that she would forward her call to a therapist. But Nancy didn't want later. She needed Maryam to listen now. So Maryam did; she listened to Nancy.

Everything Maryam had gone through the past few days fed somehow into that moment. Clean, sweep, organize, receive calls, forward calls, check up on some of the elderly living alone, sweep, break, help, call, answer, call, text, answer text, walk, dust off, shovel, clean, sweep. Sleep? People needed her. There was no time for anything else. Pressure was building and Maryam kept showing up. People needed her. People needed her. People needed her.

Nights were harder than days. Calls were more distressed then, more urgent. It was hard for Maryam to fall asleep, but at some point her body would give into the exhaustion. She felt guilty about the few hours she'd get. *What if someone needs me?* She would jolt awake and immediately check her phone.

One morning, the same person sent a message at 3 am and then again an hour later. Short messages. He was very distressed. Needed to talk. To someone. Now. And Maryam didn't wake up. She was exhausted. She couldn't wake up. She couldn't. Maryam replied back immediately. She feared she was too late. The thought was unbearable.

It was all too much.

He didn't reply that morning. She tried to keep calm and forwarded his contact to the therapists, hoping that one of them would reach out so early in the morning. One of them did, but still no reply.

She went back down to Mar Mikhael to focus on the cleanup, but she was absent, the guilt eating at her.

The man got back to the therapist early in the afternoon. He had fallen asleep. He was exhausted, after all. It was all too much.

Maryam was no longer able to stay asleep, waking up every half hour to check her phone.

Moving on

People stopped calling around a month after the hotline opened. People needed to go back to work and find a semblance of routine. Life had to move on.

At around the same time, Maryam's body could no longer cooperate, and it crashed. She was forced to take a moment to unwind. She had to rest. She had to sleep. But none of it felt right. The city was still bleeding, hearts were still broken, lives were still taken, the wounded were still injured, and the same politicians were still in power. People needed Maryam, and she needed them. She wanted to feel angry, and even waited for it to happen.

No longer preoccupied by sweeping, by cleaning, by coordinating and answering, by forwarding, consoling and listening, the sadness came crashing down. The sadness, which quickly turned into guilt, turned into numbness that was really helplessness, which became dread, then sadness all over again. But still no anger. Never anger.

After a few days of rest, she went to her new office with some friends for the first time after the explosion. After spending three weeks helping others, it was time to see what was left. As she walked into the entrance, she froze. Everything was broken, everything was gone: the sensors, the screens, the keyboards and CPUs, the windows, the doors, the frames, the lighting. There was nothing left except for a French press and a bottle of whiskey.

Washed over and overwhelmed by emotions, she could not help clean. She just couldn't. Her friend sat her down and took her broom. Maryam realized then that she, like all the people she tried to help, was also a victim.

A few hours later, on her way to her car, Maryam received a call. A woman needed help with her apartment, but there weren't many volunteers left. She had left as soon as the explosion happened. She had locked the unhinged door, walked down seven flights of stairs, found her car, and somehow managed to drive straight to the mountains. It was only now, several weeks later, that she mustered the courage to return to her completely destroyed home.

Maryam found the woman in a state of shock, washing a broken mug. She sat her down, found a broom, and began to sweep.

Written by Micha Tobia
Story contributed by Maryam Nsaif

The Emergency Room

Note: Pseudonyms have been used throughout this story.

*G*hassan *worked in a renowned hospital in Beirut for six years before being laid off, along with at least another thousand employees, in 2020, amid Lebanon's economic collapse. Ghassan was a contracted staff employee in the Emergency Department whose monthly salary was 1,100,000 Lebanese pounds, the equivalent at the time of his layoff to $137. His overtime pay was 50,000 Lebanese pounds for an eight-hour period, equivalent to $6.25 per working day. When Ghassan, thirty-three, was unceremoniously let go on October 1, the emergency room mayhem of the August 4 explosion was still fresh in his memory, as were the overtime shifts that he worked during the heaviest days of street protests, when scuffles and bloodied bodies shuffled in a steady stream for months. To Ghassan, hard work and dedication to his job in the worst of times would ensure his job security at an institution he considered home. However, during the worst economic crisis the country had faced in over a century, "home" was also where* *political interests and power struggles inside the hospital's staff syndicate played critical roles in the layoffs.*

I became a Patient Access Officer in the Emergency Department in 2014. Patients come to us as soon as they enter the Emergency Department. I worked for six years, and in these six years, many difficult moments came to pass. The August 4 explosion was a very, very painful event. It was the first time we experienced anything like it.

You should know that, during the revolution, I worked more than anyone in my division. I was the only staff member in Patient Access, along with one or two others, who slept in the hotel—because the roads were blocked, and we needed to stay nearby. I didn't see my family. I would work twenty-four hours. No other employee worked twenty-four hours. First, I loved my job. And second, there was a need and there was no one else. You could say I was senior among my colleagues of the same position, so they depended on me.

A few months before we were let go, we started hearing rumors of layoffs in our department. We have a staff syndicate. My friends are members, and they work with me in the Emergency Department. They told me, Ghassan, we have been meeting with the administration and the situation isn't good. I asked them, "What do you mean the situation isn't good?" They told me that they are going to lay off staff. And after each weekly meeting with the administration, they would tell us that the situation didn't bode well. I asked my manager about the news, but she said she didn't know anything.

Our manager is a great human being, more than you can imagine, but in difficult confrontations, she didn't manage well. To the point that the head of the Emergency Department, who is not our direct manager, stood by us more than our own manager, who was scared to lose her job. In October 2020, my contract was up. Ultimately, there was nothing to be done. The head of the Emergency Department came personally to ask about me. She was the only person who noticed how hard I worked. She stood by us. But my manager didn't.

For me, this place was my second home. I used to work at least sixteen hours a day. I was really distressed at being let go. I loved my job. I never said no. I always stayed extra when they asked.

It was just before 6:00 PM on August 4 when my wife came and saw me before going home. It was a normal day. I went out to smoke a cigarette just after she left. That's when I heard the sound of planes. I know the sound of planes because I was in the South during the July 2006 war.

Then the explosion.

Glass rained down, but luckily not on me. God saved me. I put out my cigarette and ran to the emergency room. It was destroyed. Dust was everywhere. I couldn't see anything. The sight was horrendous. You cannot imagine. One of the attendings came out, his hair was all dust. You couldn't walk inside. It was just dust, dust, dust. You couldn't see a single patient. We started emptying the emergency room. Whatever the attendings told us, we did. We moved the patients in stable condition to another floor. No one knew what was going on. Some said Hariri was killed, others said it was an Israeli attack.

My wife was still on the road. She called me crying, but I couldn't say much. I told her *hamdillah 'ssalame*, and I had to go. I was moving things and then a doctor asked me, "What's wrong? Why is your shirt all bloody?" I had no idea. He told me to go into a patient room so he could check it before anyone arrived. It turned out that glass had lodged in my back, but I didn't know. He told me I have a wound and that he'd close it for now with staples, and at the end of the night he'd stitch it properly because ambulances had started arriving.

The emergency room was a sight—the lights were hanging from the ceilings onto the floor, there was debris everywhere. We had to work together to move things and organize. Then came the injured. What can I tell you? Small children and grown men and women alike came in with wounds all over their bodies. There were people who were visiting the country and cursed the hour they came. I remember a Lebanese guy who had come from Switzerland and had been in Lebanon only two days. He didn't have anyone because his family was all abroad. His foot was broken, a bone was sticking out.

I cannot get the sights out of my mind. I was carrying a child as though she were my own daughter. Kids were walking in without their parents. Parents wanted to know where their children were. There were family members wanting to come into the surgical rooms. And they were at the doors yelling and screaming. There was security, but not enough. The hospital had to call the police and army for backup. There was fighting and breaking.

I only found out about the explosion on my phone. I checked the news quickly because we were surrounded by mayhem.

About a week after the explosion, there was the Day of Rage protest. I had just arrived home and I was tired. I had the weekend off and went to pick up a roast chicken and just wanted to have lunch with my wife and daughter. On the way, staff from Patient Access called me in three separate phone calls. They were short-handed. They said, if you come and work overtime, we can stand behind you so that they can't lay you off. Even my wife was like, "Ghassan, this is good for you. We will eat lunch together another time. Go."

That night, hundreds of patients came in. You couldn't imagine. Protesters and police, bloodied, whether due to physical fighting or beaten by truncheons or hit by tear gas canisters. We had to quickly register them. The Red Cross was bringing in tens of people at a time. We were there until ten PM. It was exhausting because we were still short-handed.

In Bedside Registration, we would take patients' IDs and their insurance cards at the door, and we were the ones who would go to their bedside and take their information so that they would not be troubled to go somewhere themselves. This is something the head of the Emergency Department insisted on so patients can be comfortable. But because we were short-handed on the night of the explosion, we couldn't register anyone in the mayhem. The president of the university ended up being furious with Patient Access. People would ask about their family members, but we didn't have the names because we were short-handed and there were tens of people flooding into the emergency room. When we asked for their IDs at the door, people became defensive and humiliated us. But we remained patient.

Yet they still closed the Bedside Registration division of the Patient Access Office. When we were let go shortly after, no one paid us any attention.

Why were some people let go and others no? It is all political. Each person has a backing. Who do you think is in the staff syndicate? It's all political parties. That's Lebanon. Everyone keeps their people. Look, I'm thirty-three years old. They let me go before a man twice my age because he is considered one of them politically. Whoever tells you no is a liar. The people who they let go were not members of any political party.

The first 500 employees to be laid off signed an agreement that they could not sign a contract with the institution again for two more years. Except for some people. Because people started leaving the country in the droves, they hired back some of those who were previously laid off. But those people got one-year contracts and they told them, "We'll see." This is exploitation. But people are desperate.

There were people who were laid off just a month before who received phone calls on August 4 to come in and help. They went to help out of humanitarian intentions. I feel they used us. They didn't care about the work we did.

We are dying every day. During elections, politicians pull our leg. I don't want to leave the country. I am my parents' only son. Anyway, I don't have the desire. I am now working part-time, four hours a day, for 500,000 lira a month. What's that, fifty dollars? There's no work. Who's going to get me a job? The political parties? Is this a salary? I was a hard worker. I never saw my family.

You know, I received an Excellent Service award. That was the first time that someone in my position was recognized. And they gave me money: $250. It was at the beginning of the collapse. That made me so happy, but it was from the Emergency Department not from the Patient Access Office. I wasn't recognized by my own division. And even though I was given an Excellent Service award, they still laid me off. Now if I had gotten the job because I was a political party member, they wouldn't have laid me off. How could they? Not one of the political party members were laid off. Their thugs would have come to the hospital and wreaked havoc.

The six of us in the Bedside Registration division weren't the only ones let go in October; there were people from housekeeping and the kitchen. Of course, they didn't lay off any doctors. They don't dare. We ended up being scapegoats. You need people to stand by you. There is a manager in nursing who took stances for her nurses. Till the end. There were four nurses who were saved by her. She fought for them. She's not scared of anyone. She ended up getting promoted. If she were our manager, maybe we would have not been let go. And even if it didn't work out, at least we would have felt that our manager supported us.

But the thing I love about this hospital is that if there's a humanitarian issue, the hospital takes care of its patients to the end. I haven't seen a hospital like this. Even though they messed up with us, I appreciate this aspect.

I still have the clothes I was wounded in on August 4. I didn't wash them. The least they can do is honor the people who worked that day, and on top of it were wounded, regardless of the size of the wound. That day, I didn't feel my wound because I wasn't thinking of myself. I didn't care. But who will shed light on this?

It was my home. I don't like to talk like this. If they asked me to go back, I would go back. But not to an exploitative and uncertain situation. They can't tell me to come work for a few months and then *later* we can talk. No. They didn't even give me a farewell. I worked with all my heart. The staff was like a family. They just told me: Good luck.

At this point, I'll work as a driver if I have to. But if you told me now to work as a driver for a political party, I would say no way, in their dreams. People who are not part of a political party treat you much better. My friend loves the Amal Movement. I asked him, why? His job pays him 800,000 lira per month. He has a mortgage, a daughter, and his wife is a teacher. I asked him, "OK, so why do you like Nabih Berri?" He said, "I like him." "But why do you like him? What has he done for you? Do you have money to pay for your generator? You sleep and sweat in the heat."

I have another friend from the Future Movement. He's been without work for one year. He's nineteen years old. Yet every year, on February 14th, he joins the protests, or he goes to Beit el-Wasat whenever there's an event. I asked him, "Did he do anything for you?" He said nothing, but that if he goes to the hospital, the party will help him with his bills. But what good is that if he doesn't have a job?

Written by Rima Rantisi
Story contributed anonymously

Degrees of Separation

At 6:00 PM on August 4, 2020, Hsein didn't even suspect he was about to embark on a grueling twelve-hour trial, a dark descent into loss.

Not even at 6:07 PM, when Hsein was in his boxers having a water fight with his young nephew on his large balcony in Aramoun. The fun and laughter stopped the second he witnessed the haunting explosion in the distance, the scene merging with memories of the July war, but on a far more monstrous scale.

Not even at 6:07 PM, when Jihane rushed onto her balcony in Naccache because of an earth-shattering sound, her eyes assaulted by an apocalyptic mushroom cloud rising from Beirut Port.

Hsein never imagined he would be navigating a maze of debris on a motorcycle and seeing pitch black misery in brightly lit hospitals.

At 6:09 PM Hsein called in to work. As the delivery manager at Zaatar w Zeit (ZwZ) in Ashrafieh near Hotel Dieu, he wanted to make sure his team members were all safe. He was crushed to hear three colleagues were seriously injured. He frantically zoomed towards Beirut, surgical mask on.

Hsein was in shock as he drove past the sad streets of Downtown and Ashrafieh. It looked like a warzone that had endured days of heavy bombardment. Hsein couldn't help recollecting disturbing memories from that tense summer in 2006 amid the shattered glass and the horror on the roads. The bloodied bodies. The stench of death and injury. Beirut reduced to rubble yet again. A city devastated so many times it was hard to keep count. *But what happened today? Pointless death, injury, and destruction that could have been totally avoided,* he thought.

He parked near his branch of ZwZ. It was unrecognizable. Only a few solitary cleaners were there, trying to erase the severe damage with brooms—an impossible feat. Hsein contacted his team, sending twenty of them out on their motorbikes to assist as many people as possible in the hardest-hit areas. He jumped on his motorcycle too. He had to do something. He had to react. Not to be a superhero. To be humane in an inhumane world.

At 6:09 PM Jihane reached for her phone, desperately trying to contact her sister, Joanna, and her brother-in-law, Ray. No one answered. Panicking, she then called the housekeeper, the concierge, and everyone else she knew who lived in her sister's neighborhood. No one answered. She threw herself in her car and drove to Beirut, maxing out the speedometer. Jihane usually drove like a turtle, but today was different. The sense of urgency made her do things out of character. Today speed limits were meant to be broken.

When Jihane got to Beirut Forum, everything stood still. A chaotic barricade of cars. She jumped out of her car and started running as fast as her arthritis let her, begging people to take her to Joanna's house next to EDL, in Mar Mikhael. Eventually, a man on a motorbike gave her a ride.

This is hell, she thought to herself. An inferno of broken glass and spattered blood. An abyss of trauma that transformed people into expressionless shells. She felt empty and zombie-like. Stressed to the point she couldn't cry or react. She prayed to wake up from this nightmare. Lost. So lost. Not sure if her sister was alive or dead. Her phone rang. Ray's cracked and worried voice told her that Joanna was seriously injured. He asked her to pick up their kids.

Jihane finally arrived. Her sister's home had been blown to bits. Distorted remnants of what it used to be. But she couldn't find her niece and nephew. So young. Only one and three. The mobile phone network was down. And so she started running without any real destination, hoping she would find them.

Amid this insanity she came across her older sister, who was also searching the streets in despair. This was when she heard that they were at Hotel Dieu. Where Joanna was. Where Ray was.

At that moment Hsein happened to be slowly inching by on his motorcycle. Jihane grabbed Hsein, pleading, "Please take me to Hotel Dieu."

"Yes, yes, yes, jump on. I'm going there." It had already been challenging for Hsein to navigate the dystopian streets, but he was ready for the additional challenge if it meant helping someone. Perhaps it was fate since they were heading to the same destination. Two strangers whose lives crossed paths unexpectedly.

This is when their snail-paced journey together began. It was just like those nightmares. The ones where monsters are in pursuit, yet you run in place, as if shackled to the ground. Only the monster was time.

They had to get to their destination quickly, but they were creeping forward so frustratingly slow. Past kids coated in dust, ash, and blood. Past the dead being covered with blankets so they could regain some dignity. Past a disheveled forty-year-old pounding his fists against a parked car shrieking, "Imagine this is your father!" while looking at a lifeless old man on the ground. Past the wounded getting stitched and treated on the road outside an overflowing small hospital by overwhelmed doctors and nurses already drained by the COVID-19 pandemic.

The road was hidden under a sea of concrete chunks, stone fragments, metal rods, groaning bodies, crimson blood, and beaten-up cars. Collapsed buildings were on both sides. Time was cruelly ticking in the real world, but in their minds, each second felt like hours. The commotion around them was deafening. And yet their ears were deaf to the commotion and weeping around them. They could only hear their own panicked breathing.

There was no escape. All the side streets that led out of Mar Mikhael were inaccessible, blockaded by pulverized cars and broken people. Motorcycles could barely squeeze past. They couldn't go up. They couldn't go down. They couldn't turn left. They couldn't turn right.

Hsein and Jihane edged forward one millimeter at a time in silence, barely exchanging words. Jihane, consumed by thoughts about her sister. Hsein, eaten away by worry about a dear colleague who was in critical condition, and whose whereabouts were unknown. Anxious numbness permeated every cell of their beings. Escape, that's all they wanted. Time was mercilessly speeding by while they were trapped, hearts racing, breath uneven.

After what felt like an eternity, they managed to break free into Tabaris and could finally drive at full speed. This moment of elation evaporated in an instant though. Slivers of broken glass were everywhere, waiting to rip the tires to shreds. Jihane's surgical mask flew away in a strong gust. They zigzagged their way to Albergo Hotel, the darkness enveloping them. The flickering streetlights suggested there was light at the end of the tunnel.

Then the motorcycle broke down, stubbornly refusing to move.

"Please no," beseeched Hsein. Jihane got off the bike saying, "Don't worry, I can walk the rest of the way. Thanks for all your help." She had to get to Hotel Dieu. It didn't matter how.

"No, it's too far. I will drop you off at the hospital's entrance," insisted Hsein, as he closely examined the bike. He removed the iron rod lodged in the wheel spoke and they continued their journey.

Jihane's phone rang, the sound piercing the silence.

"Come quickly. Jo is bleeding a lot and is unconscious. It's not looking good," wailed Ray. Jihane crumbled, hysterical with worry. Hsein tried to calm her down.

"Everything will be OK. It will be fine. Things will be better by tomorrow. You'll see." Hsein could sense the swell of darkness rushing through Jihane's mind. He knew how devastating this would be had he been in her shoes, worrying about his mother or sister.

Hotel Dieu was finally in view. Jihane got off and started running. Before she disappeared in the dense crowds Hsein shouted, "I work at Zaatar w Zeit. Please call me tomorrow to update me on your sister."

Jihane thanked Hsein profusely for his kindness.

"In moments like these, you really don't need to thank me," he replied.

Jihane teared up.

The hospital was total anarchy. Dashing through the mad corridors, Jihane finally found Ray and Joanna. She was thankful Ray wasn't injured and the kids were miraculously untouched. But Joanna's condition was heart-wrenching and extremely critical.

Jihane discovered what had transpired. The building Ray and Joanna called home was directly hit by the blast. Ray found Joanna under heavy debris soaked in blood, her cheek completely blown away. It was a struggle to carry Joanna to the building's entrance. Ray started screaming frantically for help as blood continued to gush out of Joanna. She was barely breathing. A stranger in a half-destroyed car rushed to their aid. The young man took off his red shirt and covered Joanna's wounded face, red on red. The car roof was so dented that it was impossible to open the doors, so Ray and the young man had to carefully slide Joanna into the car. The young man drove like he was possessed, driving on the sidewalk without any concern for the further damage he was inflicting on his car. As soon as he dropped them off at Hotel Dieu, he took off and was soon out of sight.

Joanna was shaking and screaming, slipping in and out of consciousness in a half-coma. But the very next day, Ray started looking for the mysterious young man by asking around and through social media. The young man was also looking, too, for "Jo," even going to their building to ask the neighbors.

The mysterious stranger was no stranger at all. They say everyone is connected by six degrees of separation, but he was connected by just one. Jihane was best friends with the young man's mother, Leila. The young man, Taha, knew Jihane very well, and loved the cakes she baked him over the years.

At around noon the next day, Jihane called ZwZ and left Hsein a message. Hsein called her back ten minutes later. He was sad to learn that Joanna had a long and tough recovery ahead of her, but he was also relieved to hear her surgery went well. To cheer Jihane up, Hsein sent a *choco-banane man'oushe* and juice to Hotel Dieu. He couldn't bear to go in person. He knew he couldn't take seeing more people wavering between life and death. He was still reeling from the horrendous sights and lingering exhaustion from last night. That dreadful sleepless night. Filled with the whirlwind emotions of all the people who were on his bike.

Hsein and Jihane stayed in touch long after and were fascinated by the coincidences. How they were at the same place at the same time, heading toward the same destination. How they both worked in F&B and were the same age. How they had attended the same events in the past, and their lives had crossed paths many times before they actually met that night.

But Hsein's night didn't end after dropping off Jihane. He went back to his ZwZ branch. His severely injured colleague had been tracked down to a hospital. "Thank goodness he's alive and has been found," sighed Hsein. He checked on each of the motorcyclists he had sent out, one by one. They were busy taking people from hospital to hospital, as most were full. Hsein felt compelled to hit the streets again, too.

While driving down Bechara El Khoury, Hsein saw a ghost of a man covered in blood, hobbling rather than walking. He took him to Rizk Hospital. Hsein never learned the man's name or found out who he was. He simply focused on helping. Tires turning. Engine purring. Wind blowing. Everything was a blur.

The phone rang, bringing Hsein back to reality.

"My brother was at Beirut Port during the explosion and is now at Rizk Hospital. Please find our other sibling, Ramez. He should be at the hospital watching over our injured brother," his sister-in-law pleaded. Fate had it that Hsein was already at Rizk. It was total turmoil inside the hospital. Like nothing he had ever seen before. Throngs of people, eyes filled with confusion, in postures of helplessness and frustration. Hsein anxiously searched from floor to floor. Out of breath. The smell of blood, sweat, and disinfectant assaulting his nostrils. The phone rang. His sister-in-law said Ramez had been found. Relief.

Hsein left Rizk Hospital. Before he could even think of his next destination, his phone rang. It was a colleague asking for Hsein's help in tracking down a man called Jacques. Hsein contacted his team so they could help, but they couldn't find Jacques amid the pandemonium. His phone rang again. It was Elianna, another colleague. She also wanted to find Jacques, who was her brother-in-law. On his way to pick up Elianna from Mar Mitr, his phone rang. A driver had found Jacques.

A few moments later Hsein and Elianna were speeding towards Sahel Hospital on the motorbike. Both were so immersed in their thoughts they couldn't see or hear anything during the ride. Hsein didn't know how to tell Elianna that Jacques was dead. The only words that escaped his mouth were "Jacques is at Sahel Hospital." Hsein was confused and conflicted. His mind was in overdrive: "How can I break the news when we get to the hospital? It's so awful." Mayhem greeted them at Sahel. And the rotten stench of despair. Hsein inquired about Jacques. A frazzled health care professional took them to one side and told them he was dead. Elianna broke down in tears. As a colleague rather than a friend, Hsein wasn't sure how to comfort Elianna. He knew nothing could ease her raw pain, so he did the only thing he could do. He held her as she wept. He then gave her a cigarette and a warm cup of coffee.

A few minutes later they were asked if they wanted to see the body. Elianna wanted to. She had to see. To make sure it was true. To say goodbye. The bleak morgue, with its line of drawers, was chilling. An unusual putrid odor seemed to seep from the walls. A jaundiced hue lit the room. They opened a drawer. And there he was. Elianna cried uncontrollably. With fumbling hands, she called her husband in the UAE, sobbing while sharing the heartbreaking news. This was all incredibly tough for Hsein. Witnessing Elianna's grief. Dealing with the sights and sounds thundering through the hospital. Seeing the corpse. The harsh reality of meeting someone for the first time, when they're already shrouded in death's mask. Only to later meet Jacques in life through photos. This handsome, kind, and fun person. They had many common friends and acquaintances. And yet their paths only crossed when it was too late.

Hsein took Elianna home and then drove to his own place in Aramoun. By the time he arrived it was six in the morning. The whole experience had been so mentally draining that he couldn't sleep. He didn't even notice the toll the events left on his body. Scenes from that never-ending night kept replaying in his mind. Remembering the wells of tears and the isolated, awkward smiles of traumatized people, he sat there on his balcony in a stupor, just smoking, drinking coffee, and sighing. No one slept that night. But fate brought some strangers together in their hour of need, with just a degree of separation.

Written by Jasmina Najjar
Story contributed by Jihane Dagher Hayeck and Hsein Kashmar

New Beginnings

In Karm el-Joz in the fall, the evening wind rushing between the walnut trees howled almost too ominously for joyful celebration. The hundreds of baby roses, daisies, and wildflowers Melissa placed in glass vases across wooden tables added a sweet aroma to the chilling breeze at the entrance of the Bekaa Valley orchard. Her best friend, Alexandra, wanted an Italian countryside vintage-style wedding, with a modern twist and an outdoor church. And Melissa had done just that. After hours of working with suppliers to set up the bar, floor, and lighting, everything came together with the fantasy she envisioned.

Standing on the grass ten meters away from the outdoor dining tables, she watched a man in his thirties dressed in black-and-white attire help himself to pieces of Gouda, Boursin, and Brie from a cheese platter while telling a story that sent a crowd into uproarious laughter. She looked at the happy faces and imagined the compliments she would receive from the newlyweds. "You've given us the best night of our lives," she hoped they would say.

After seven years, she had won the hard-earned trust and mutual respect of the best suppliers and vendors her small country had to offer. Her identity, for those who barely knew her, was constructed entirely on her enviable profession: Melissa the talented wedding planner.

Not every wedding was as fun and seamless as her best friend's. As the makeup on her face started to melt under the Mediterranean sun, she was shaken back to a memory from the year before.

Despite all her experience, she had never planned a wedding with as many prospective food and beverage choices as the groom's father, a businessman, wanted: tastings with chefs, mixologists, a late-night menu... It was all beyond extravagant. So, when he haggled her over a mere fifty-dollar price difference on one item, she nearly spit out her water in his face.

"I'm sorry, I have already brought down the price as much as I can," she said.

She was used to negotiating, but never expected it to be so tireless with a man who had amassed a literal empire. Like an octopus, he had tentacles in many sectors of Lebanon's economy. She felt sick to her stomach, and seriously contemplated yielding to his demand, just to rid herself of him as quick as she could. But she stood her ground.

"I've already gone back and forth with the vendors many times for you. I would be paying for it myself," she said.

The business mogul rolled up his sleeves and bellowed in what appeared to be his most threatening tone: "Do you know who I am?"

"I don't care who you are," Melissa retorted, unflinchingly.

The businessman, who had been expecting the usual acquiescence, was suddenly caught off guard. His face reddened.

There are people starving in the streets, she thought, recalling the sight of boys searching through dumpsters behind Beirut's most bustling commercial district. *And here is an affluent man who is literally haggling me over a fifty-dollar difference.*

All at once, the man rose and left, slamming the door on his way out.

She boiled inside remembering the event. Yet the evening breeze brought her back to the joyous occasion in Karm el-Joz. *How much longer can you take it here?* it seemed to whisper.

On the third floor of Hotel Dieu hospital's ward in an Eastern Beirut neighbor-hood, friends and strangers surrounded Ayman al-Dakdouk with flowers and chocolates, waiting for word as to whether he would lose his sight. He had been in the midst of clashes between protesters and security forces the night before. He was carrying a young girl out of harm's way when a riot police threw a rock that bloodied his eye. He was rushed to the hospital and lay in bed in a white gown with an October 17th button on his chest. Melissa was among the crowd surrounding Ayman's bedside. She was there in lieu of the government. She was there to support her fellow protesters. Days like this made her worry even more about her country's fate and her own. Her savings were quickly diminishing, and there seemed to be an insurmountable force preventing the revolution from materializing. Her middle sister had long settled in the United States, and the youngest had recently moved there with her husband, whose visa was only just approved. Her mother began putting pressure on her to leave, too. Unlike most people trapped in the country, Melissa had US citizenship, which allowed her to easily escape. But she was not ready. She was the type of person who takes life day by day, and on that day, she was not ready to give up hope.

On August 4, 2020, Melissa joined a protest crowd of over five hundred people in front of the Energy Ministry. It had been ten months since Lebanon's revo-lution had erupted, and she decided to take to the streets at every opportunity she could. It had been six months since she last planned a wedding.

With the various COVID-related government-imposed lockdowns, the protest movement had stagnated. She still went out to the streets when she could, but also turned her energy to Baytna Baytak ("our home is your home"), an NGO born in March to provide alternative housing for front-line health workers in order to protect their families.

Despite the pause that COVID imposed on life in Lebanon, public dis-content was still as strong as ever, with prolonged power cuts being one of the many sources of frustration. On that sweltering August day, people emerged back to the streets to voice their anger, the same anger that had consumed Melissa, who had long witnessed corruption in her years of wedding planning for the rich and powerful.

She met up with her friend Ayman Raad, a forty-year-old, burly, always clean-shaven defendant of the Lawyers' Committee for the Defense of

Protesters (LCDP) at the demo. His face was perpetually alert, and he looked like he could be a government official or be cast as a lead detective in a mystery film. Like Melissa, Ayman was on the ground since the beginning of the protests, and they first met in the crucible of the revolution. Acting as sort-of vigilantes mediating between the Internal Security Forces (ISF) and citizens, Ayman and other LCDP lawyers interfered when excessive force was used, which was often. Mass arrests and gratuitous violence came to characterize the Lebanese government during the uprising, with over 1,200 people detained for merely participating.

Shortly after catching up, Ayman followed a group of ten protesters lined up in a row on a narrow island dividing a main street, attracting the attention of the ISF. When they approached him, he confidently exclaimed, "Don't touch me, I'm a lawyer."

He knew that the officers did not have the right to use force on *anyone*, but being a lawyer gave him a sort of shield. This time, the leverage failed and an officer forcefully pushed him. Ayman instinctually slapped him back and a scuffle ensued. He was brought to the ground—hard. A former boxer, Melissa rushed over to pull the security forces off him, her tiger instinct kicking in. The next thing she knew, she was slapped hard across the face, so hard it sent her sunglasses flying and turned her head to the side. She lost her mind.

"*Ibn sharmouta*! You son of a bitch! Whichever coward slapped me, come out and face me now!"

The lieutenant responsible for the officers approached her, trying to reconcile on behalf of the group. "I'm sorry, *anti akhti wa anti 'ala rasi*. You're my sister and I'd do anything for you," he said endearingly. But Melissa would have none of it. She wanted the security forces to understand that they were putting themselves in a terrible position by defending the wrong people.

While indignation had been her predominant emotion during the revolution, she felt, for the first time, a helpless sadness. "Look at what we've become," she screamed. "Don't you understand, we're the ones paying the price!"

It took her a while before she realized that her favorite Ray-Bans were missing, but when she did, she went back to the spot where the officer slapped her and started looking. The sunglasses meant so much to her. They had accompanied her to every protest and became ingrained in her transformation from wedding planner to activist. She looked under cars, on the sidewalks, on the streets and highways for what felt like hours, but to no avail. Drenched in sweat, she returned home to quickly change her clothes.

At any other day at 6:00 PM, before COVID disrupted the world's routine, she would have been working, or in a wedding meeting, or at the gym, or volunteering to support people in need, or, of course, protesting. Instead, for the first time in what felt like a lifetime, she was at home when her phone screen went black. *That's strange,* she thought. As she headed towards the router, the balcony doors suddenly swelled in, like giant bubbles about to attack her. At exactly 6:07 PM, she was swept up off her feet and tossed backward across the room. The entire building shook. In her apartment no glass broke, not even a wine glass, since the windows were open.

She ran out onto the streets as fast as she could. It took what felt like a long time before she learned that the blast was not nearby but several kilometers away at the port. That was when she suddenly understood the scale of the death and destruction that had just struck her city. In that moment she felt ironically awakened, the sort of alive you feel when you wake up in the morning, open the shades, and are blinded by the bright light. She didn't know what to make of the feeling, what to make of the mixed cloak of invincibility and stimulation that wrapped her, blinded her perhaps. All she knew was that she had no time to think about it. She had to provide help.

Melissa shouted to her cousin Oussama that she needed a motorcycle and fast. He told her that her second cousin Samir, whom she had not seen since he was a child, had a bike.

Within minutes, Samir showed up on a black-and-silver Honda CB300. She hoped that he would allow her to take the lead and drive her around for the night, so that she could deliver first aid to as many in need as possible.

"Where are we going?" Samir asked in a soft voice. He had a shaved head and wore a plain black hoodie. "I'm at your service."

As Melissa hopped on the bike, she couldn't help thinking that she should be planning a wedding right now. It's what any wedding planner did during the summer.

When it rains in Beirut, the rain is so heavy that it hurts to be hit by the drops. The rain, as Mellissa's dad used to tell her growing up, meant that God was purifying the dirty city, preparing her to become beautiful. It was a cold and rainy winter day when Melissa decided to sit on her balcony and look out at the stormy city.

As she watched people with umbrellas and ponchos cross the streets, she thought, *Was it the explosion that gave me purpose? And does that purpose mean that it was a good thing it happened?* She gasped. "Thank God no one can read my thoughts," she uttered beneath her breath, clutching her cardboard cup filled with lukewarm Nescafe. Her stomach growled.

A meowing black cat, appropriately named Cat, jumped on her lap and purred as she pet her. She was suddenly jolted back to August, that wretched day bludgeoned into the memory of every Lebanese. While the rain poured down, she was swept by a whirlwind of self-reproach and nostalgic anger.

She felt a pang of regret for taking Samir through the smoky scenes of Gemmayze and Mar Mikhael, where lampposts hung, electricity cables sprawled on the floors, and buildings collapsed around them. They had spent most of the evening in and outside Serhal Hospital, delivering blood to patients and trying not to be sick from the horrific scenes involving blood and broken bodies. She remembered the emaciated face of a nearly decapitated elderly woman whose life, the accumulation of decades in Lebanon, had been forever robbed of dignity.

Melissa remembered the absurd moment when she tapped Samir's shoulder, only after having driven around piles upon piles of rubble and shards, and asked, "How bad are we ruining your tires?" She remembered returning home at 2:30 AM on August 4, exhausted after riding around the city with Samir. She could not find Cat but needed to urgently begin cleaning. She worked in the food industry long enough to know that some of the 2,750 tons of ammonium nitrate that had exploded had certainly made its way into the building, despite it being kilometers away.

Nour, her roommate, had driven through the epicenter of the explosion on her way home from work, and the experience had been traumatic. She silently emerged from her room to help look for Cat and clean up. They remained silent, showering the apartment with buckets of water, until Nour went to the Bluetooth speaker and put on some Arabic party trap. In that moment, they were swept up by Muhammad Ramadan's lyrics on repeat and lifelessly danced while cleaning into the dead of the night. Part of them, like every other Lebanese, had perished that evening. After the deep clean, they put on a couple of episodes of *Friends*, trying to distract themselves from their hellish reality. At around six that morning, they flopped into their beds but could barely close their eyes. Cat was still missing, swaths of the city had been annihilated, and thousands were homeless.

Melissa awoke around 8 AM with a strong desire to do something, anything, to help, knowing that, once again, the government certainly wouldn't. She awoke with a massive headache, chugged coffee until she felt the caffeine in her veins, threw on a tank top and ripped jeans, and headed out the door.

The morning after the explosion, millions of shards and particles of glass lay spilled across Beirut. All at once, the early stillness was transformed into an orchestra of brooms sweeping glass across streets, until the sound rose into a crescendo, lasting for hours.

Flashbulb memories snuck up out of nowhere, like that time Melissa had Sunday brunch with her mother at Home Sweet Home, or the New Year's Eve party where eighty friends gathered at Bohemian two years before, or when she had helped close down a road in anger at the corruption.

Hours passed as Melissa swept her way through the streets to Electricité du Liban. She appeared on *France 24*, a French state-owned international news network, speaking in an angry, defiant voice about how she had led volunteers to throw the debris and garbage in front of the electricity company. It only seemed natural to turn the company into a dumpster, a symbol of the rampant corruption that had blown up in their faces.

Melissa was filled with a mix of rage and sorrow—but she also felt lucky. She hadn't lost anyone, nor did she have any material damages. She even found Cat. But some of her close ones were not so lucky, like Maroun, friend, fellow activist, and co-founder of Baytna Baytak. When he called the next day, they agreed to meet on the rooftop of his dilapidated building, which was filled with fancy furnished apartments only the day before.

Tall and broad-shouldered, Maroun always wore a brown or black Fedora. He liked to laugh and cared about looking good, always sporting a well-groomed beard, white button-down shirt, and Apple watch. The night before, he had lost two friends in the blast and had himself been wounded, in his leg. Yet he barely gave himself time to grieve. Even in the face of tragedy, he had an exceptionally positive attitude.

Standing on the rooftop with seven friends from Baytna Baytak, the world sweeping below them, Melissa felt clarity, the most she had felt in a long time. She inhaled and heaved a doleful sigh, nervously looking for a cigarette before declaring, "If there was any hope of me leaving before the explosion, there is absolutely no hope of me leaving now."

The houses that Baytna Baytak had provided as shelter for doctors and nurses were badly damaged from the blast, so rebuilding them was a natural next step.

Vacation. What the hell does that mean? The thought irked her. Since Melissa had taken on the responsibility of vice president at Baytna Baytak, she had been lucky to sleep a few hours a night. Work followed her to the bedroom, and she led a team of over ninety employees who served hundreds of families.

Her days and nights consisted of phone calls. Just in the past day, a nurse needed housing, a sick man needed an oxygen machine, and an elderly woman needed medicine. While she was involved in new beginnings before—marrying people off—her "new beginnings" now involved giving families homes.

The methods were the same: delegating tasks, communicating effectively, networking, following up, and inspiring trust in her team and clients. But now, she had found the purpose she had been lacking in her almost unrecognizable life as a wedding planner. Now she made a difference that could be quantified by the number of houses she helped rebuild.

The number of cigarettes she smoked had also increased, she thought, while taking a puff at the beach. It was mid-May and Eid al-Fitr, marking the end of the holy month of Ramadan. Her friends forced her to the beach with them. The sun had been unusually hot that month. Yet on this particular breezeless day, a disappointing overcast covered the sky, giving her a mere few minutes of sunlight before disappearing, as if telling her, "Get back to work!" She looked down at her phone and saw 250 unread messages since she had tried to doze off only ten minutes ago.

Melissa lay back in her beach chair. The sun finally shone on her skin, and with that, a sense of anxiety edged its way into her. Her headache started once again, but she couldn't pin down what exactly was bothering her. She had, after all, changed so much in the past year, and for the better: "aesthetics," friends, habits, life philosophy and priorities. On the outside, she was still strong and fierce, just as she had always been. Except now she was no longer a wedding planner but a humanitarian, deeply committed to her country's political and social future. As she lay under the sun, she suddenly realized what was bothering her. A question popped into her mind, one that she had never articulated before, certainly not during her days as a wedding planner. She let out a big sigh: *How much more can I keep giving my ravenous country until it devours me?*

Written by AJ Naddaff
Story contributed by Melissa Fathallah

III. ON SOLIDARITY

The Purse

This story does not begin at 6:07 PM on August 4, 2020, but several hours earlier, the morning of that warm summer day. It does not start at the port of Beirut either, nor in any other part of the Lebanese capital. This story begins simultaneously in two mountain locations outside the city.

It is 7:30 AM at a camping site in Chahtoul, a village in the mountains north of Beirut. Angelique gives in to the inevitable, opens her tent zipper, and gets out, having barely slept an hour. She had come from Beirut the evening before with a bottle of rosé and some rolling tobacco to spend the night alone under the light of the full moon. Her night was restless for reasons she could not understand.

Angelique decides to drive back to Beirut. It is a working day, and she has meetings lined up all afternoon. She thinks about canceling them at first, considering how little she's slept, but she decides to stick to her plan and head somewhere to work.

129

She drives back to Beirut along the road that leads down to the coast. The closer she gets to the city, the more cars begin to crowd the road. It is still a comparatively smooth drive. The hour is early, and the inevitable jams are yet to materialize. When she reaches the city, she heads straight to Sip, a coffee shop with mosaic floors and large windows overlooking the main street of Gemmayze, not far from the city center. She pushes the door open to enter, sees that her favorite table next to the door is empty, and takes a seat.

In a mountain town outside of Beirut, Elias awakens. He is visiting Lebanon with his sister. They live in France but they have family and relatives here. They spontaneously visit for a couple of days at a time whenever they can manage it. The last time they were both in Lebanon together was 2006, in the dead heat of summer. Elias was twelve, and his sister ten. He remembers landing in the midst of the World Cup craze. France was playing, and his aunts let him dye his hair *bleu, blanc, et rouge* in support of the team. During that trip, his tween self was twice shocked: first, by the defeat of the French team by the Italians in the final, then by the sudden war with Israel. *I stopped being a child that summer,* he thinks to himself, understanding that this unpredictability is why his father decided to leave the country so many years ago.

Elias drives north. He leaves his family's house near Saida in southern Lebanon and heads to Zahle, a town at the bottom of the mountains overlooking the Bekaa Valley, where more family live. He heads out early in the morning because he knows a mechanic with a garage there. His car had made a strange noise the night before, and, more important, he discovered the AC was not working.

It is still early when he reaches the small valley town, so he decides to take a quick nap. He didn't sleep well, or much, after a long night of partying. He wakes up to a text from his aunt: "I took the car but will be back shortly." Elias texts her back: "Please check if the AC is working. Something seems to be wrong with it." A few hours later, she returns with the car, hands over the keys, and tells him that she fixed the AC. Elias takes them, starts the car, and drives down to Beirut.

At Sip, Angelique orders a late lunch but hardly touches her plate. She still feels nauseated from the night before, which is strange since nothing in particular happened. She continues her meetings and finishes early, before half past four. She has a few different options for the rest of the afternoon: go to Hamra, on the other side of town, to pick something up for her mum, or head straight to an event planned for that evening, a bit outside Beirut, to the north. Enough time passes to make the decision for her and she ends up staying at Sip.

When Elias reaches the coast, the car is as warm as the summer air outside. He quickly realizes that the AC wasn't fixed, turns it off, and opens all the windows instead.

It is lunchtime when he arrives to Gemmayze, where he booked a room for himself and his sister. Today is her birthday. Just before reaching the hotel, he passes by one of his favorite cafés in the city, Sip, with a facade of big windows and a constantly revolving door.

Elias picks up his sister and takes her on a tour of Beirut, stopping at all his favorite spots. The city has changed since they were last in it together as kids. When the afternoon is just about to turn into evening, the siblings decide to head north, out of the city, for a drink somewhere by the sea.

They drive through Gemmayze and pass by Sip once more. The sun is strong and it is hard to see through the windows, but the place is clearly filled with people sitting alone or in small groups.

"We have to get breakfast here tomorrow," Elias tells his sister.

Inside Sip, Angelique is still at her table by the window. There are two girls next to her, sitting face-to-face. It is six, and Angelique still has some time to kill before her event at seven.

The sharp sound of a plane flying very, very low breaks the melodious coffee shop murmur. Then there are two loud strikes. Everyone in the café and outside on the small patio starts to panic.

"Is this what I think it is?" one of the girls next to Angelique asks out loud.

"I guess so, but I hope not," she finds herself replying.

"Then why are we still seated and not running?" the girl says.

This is enough to get everyone up. Angelique reaches for her purse, just next to her on the bench near the glass window, when a blast of air throws her with tornado force back into her seat. She hears a massive explosion, and a thick cloud of brown dust enters the café. Angelique feels nothing.

Elias and his sister have almost reached Dawra, the big roundabout on the northern outskirts of the city. The junction is busy with taxis and cars coming from all directions, trying to overtake loitering buses. The siblings find themselves stuck behind a red-plated taxi.

The driver starts driving exceedingly slow and reaches his arm out through the window to film something. At first, Elias does not notice anything strange. He is so caught up with the plans for the evening, as is his sister.

Suddenly everything around them slows down, much slower than usual. Not just the taxi in front of them, but every car, on all sides. Nothing tangible, nothing that they can see, has happened; there's just a strange kind of heaviness and tension in the air. Elias's phone pings with a text from his aunt: "Something small has exploded in Beirut but don't worry." Elias taps the screen to get back to the clock on the main screen. It is 6:04 PM.

It is only then that they notice the smoke blanketing the sky behind them. With each second, it grows heavier and more imposing.

"Here we go again, another war," Elias's sister says, the words emerging gradually from her mouth while the smoke grows thicker.

"No, it's coming from the port," Elias says. "Something must be burning in the heat."

Through force of will, Angelique manages to get her body up off the chair and rises to her feet. Immediately she feels something warm run down the right side of her face. There is no pain, just the sensation of a slow trickle. She can hear a voice calling from the dust inside the café: "Go to the Red Cross, they are just across the street." She stumbles outside, almost immediately realizing that she's left her purse and laptop behind. She turns back inside and sees one of the waiters in the same state of shock.

"Go, I will keep your things safe," he tells her.

She makes her feet step outside again, leaving the chaos of the café for the havoc in the street. The warm liquid keeps streaming down her face. It drips like a slow, unhesitating rill in spring. She assumes that it is coming from the side of her head but cannot locate where. She is focused on one thing and one thing only: finding medical help.

The cloud behind Elias and his sister keeps growing, like a monster eating up everything in its path. Elias glances at his sister, certain she is trying to tell him something, but he cannot hear a word. He loses control of the car for a moment, then manages to make it stop and turns off the engine. Cars around them are also stopping, many with windows entirely blown out. A big store window next to them is in pieces. Everything seems to be happening either in slow motion or extremely sped up.

Elias looks at his sister again. She looks back without a word. They both realize that nothing has happened to them; they are fine.

Angelique starts the long walk from Sip through the now devastated main street of Gemmayze. She reaches the Red Cross just across the way, but it is in the same state as all the other buildings lining the street: destroyed.

"We have no supplies. We can't even move our ambulance. Try Wardieh Hospital instead."

Angelique backtracks. Wardieh is in the other direction. She reaches the hospital only to find it shattered as well.

"There's nothing left here, the place is completely destroyed. Try Geitawi Hospital."

She hesitates and freezes. Geitawi is farther away, up a small hill at the end of Gemmayze. It would not have been a long walk on any normal day, but today it seems to take an eternity.

A young man approaches her. "Come on," he says. "We have to walk. We have no other choice." His words, his presence and company give her the strength to continue.

Blood continues to flow down the side of her face and starts making its way past her lips and into her mouth. She tries not to swallow but finds it impossible to walk and keep the blood from trickling down her throat.

The young man only has socks on his feet. The road is entirely covered with pieces of glass and metal, like a bed of shrapnel and diamonds, as if everything that could possibly have broken around them did. They keep walking, having lost any sense of time. How long has it been—minutes or hours?

The moment Elias meets his sister's gaze, it hits him. The AC wasn't on. They were driving with their windows open, which is why they still had them.

Elias is bombarded with thoughts: *What happened? Will it be like in 2006? We didn't see it coming. Are we safe or is this just the beginning?* He can hear his father telling him as a kid growing up in France, "If anything happens in Beirut, go north. You'll be safe there."

Elias always hated that civil war thinking, stemming from trauma and old protection mechanisms: If you're Christian, go north. If you're Muslim, go south. Considering where they were, there was nothing else they could do. They were going north because nothing behind them was safe.

All his life, Elias tried to protect the people around him from danger and threat. He texts his dad: "Hey, we're having a drink at a beach bar by the sea. Am running out of battery so don't worry if I don't reply." The intention was not to lie, but to spare his dad worry until they knew more. The phone pings back immediately: "How dare you lie to me! Where are you? Are you safe? I saw what happened, just drive and don't go back."

The walk through Gemmayze and up the hill to Geitawi somehow comes to an end. Angelique finds herself standing outside the hospital. Only when she reaches the door does she see that everything is destroyed. There is no light inside and the ceiling has collapsed.

"There's nothing here. You need to go to another hospital," someone tells her.

Angelique feels her legs and knees weaken. Everyone around her looks lost or confused, moving aimlessly like zombies. Two women walk by filming with their phone. Some people hurry past, others sit down wherever they can and wait.

A man comes up to her. "What do you need?" he asks.

"I have to stop the bleeding," she says. "I need to get to a hospital."

"What is your blood type?" he asks. "Your name, your age?"

He doesn't believe her when she says she is thirty-nine, until she gives him her phone and the four-digit unlock code, and tells him to reply to any calls.

The man leaves and soon returns. "I have found an ambulance," he says. "Come. We will go to another hospital."

The ambulance is almost full when they get there. An elderly woman sits on a folding seat. Others stand close to each other. A young girl, only a couple of years old, lies on the stretcher. They keep calling her name over and over to keep her from passing out: "Alexandra! Alexandra!"

The siblings listen to their dad and continue driving. When they reach Jounieh, they stop at a bar somewhere near the sea. They wait. They have two cold margaritas and eat way too many carrots soaked in lemon juice. Wait. They check in on everyone they know, calling friends, family, relatives, friends of friends. They listen to stories, rumors, theories and speculations from anyone in the bar. Then they decide to drive back to the city.

The ambulance leaves Geitawi but hardly gets anywhere. The roads are mayhem, filled with cars, too many cars, that all need to go somewhere.

"It is going to be a long ride. All hospitals from here to Baabda are full," the driver says.

Angelique's memory gets hazy at this point. She remembers reaching Hotel Dieu, which is normally only a short drive from Geitawi. She recalls entering the hospital and being taken to a hallway teeming with people on beds and floors, arriving to another hallway, moving to another building, and hearing a voice say, "Get her to Dr. Okais. Take her to one of the rooms on the left."

It has been dark for several hours by the time Elias and his sister start the drive back to Beirut. When they reach the outskirts of the city, the first thing they see is the Forum de Beyrouth. The facade is blown away, leaving a bare, bent, and broken metal skeleton. The air feels thick and heavy to breathe. The siblings take out the masks they have lying around—pandemic accessories—and put them on. Elias tries to park the car at the Total Medawar station facing the Forum but is unable to. He can't remember how to park. An old man in the street laughs at his attempt to reverse.

His phone keeps pinging with messages telling him to go back north, to not return to the city. But Elias just has to return.

Hours after Angelique's arrival, Dr. Okais has stitched up all of her wounds: the one above her right eye, the other on her nose, and several on her forehead.

Her brother and cousin come to the hospital. They start showing her video clips of the blast's aftermath, videos filmed from balconies of high buildings showing the massive gray cloud. Seeing the blast, the scenes in the streets, she starts naming people she knows, people living or working near the port. Her cousin calls them one after the other. They are safe.

Elias and his sister arrive at Armenia Street, the road connecting Dawra to Gemmayze. They had thought the Forum de Beyrouth was the worst hit, but they couldn't have been more wrong. The farther down the street they go, the more destruction they see. Everything has been turned upside down, thrown aside, torn apart.

Elias sees a body being pulled out from the remains of a house.

"Don't look!" he screams to his sister. It is like being back in 2006, having to look after her again.

They leave the car—it's impossible to drive—and start walking in the direction of the hotel. Everything feels surreal. The road is entirely covered in glimmering glass, giving voice to each broken step.

They finally reach the hotel and are about to open the door when something catches Elias's eye. A bag, lying on the street just outside Sip. The purse, filled with books, pens, and an iPad, seems precious, the only recognizable thing in the midst of all this destruction. Elias picks it up and they leave.

It is dawn when Angelique wakes up. She changes into the clean clothes her mum sent to the hospital and walks through the hallways, still full of people waiting their turn to be stitched up. She heads to the ground floor and leaves.

Elias and his sister head straight to Zahle from Gemmayze, reaching the small mountain town in the middle of the night. They unpack their things. Elias takes out all the contents of the bag from outside Sip and places them on the floor: *Where is the owner of the bag now? What happened to her? If I manage to find her, what will I discover?*

He starts looking for a clue, any clue to help him figure out who she is. And then, on a piece of paper, there it is, a name: Angelique S.

The days that follow are like a long continuation of what happened. Angelique recovers from her injury, but the city remains shattered.

She feels better a couple of days later and goes back to Gemmayze. The concierge of the building behind Sip has her laptop and power bank, but her purse is nowhere to be found.

A week after the explosion, at a memorial for the victims, Angelique immediately recognizes three people who were with her in the ambulance, the parents and grandfather of Alexandra. (Alexandra Naggear, three, and Isaac Oehlers, two, were the youngest victims of the Beirut explosion.)

Elias finally finds an Instagram account and sends a message. He also uploads a story on his own feed: "Please share. I found this purse in the rubble in Gemmayze. It belongs to Angelique S. I hope she is safe. If anyone knows her, please let me know."

Angelique's friend Eric sends her a message: "Someone I know just posted this on Instagram. He is looking for you. He has your bag."

Angelique and Elias decide to meet at the Total Medawar station for the handover. Elias parks his car almost exactly where he tried to park that night, the northern highway behind him and the port on the horizon. There is no smoke rising from the harbor, only the rods and ruins of buildings blown away.

Elias hands her the purse. They exchange a few words about what happened, how indescribable it was. It's strange, but they feel like they already know each other.

Elias thinks about the summer of 2006, about being twelve, his little sister ten. He sees Angelique as a sister, as someone he has to protect. He can see that she is out of danger but not yet OK. She needs time to heal.

Written by Jenny Gustafsson
Story contributed by Angelique and Elias

137

Two Streets Over

Hassan

Hassan held his breath as he stacked the final stone on his sculpture, the rocks tumbling the minute he let go. He put the stones back where he found them and headed home, turning his back to the asparagus fields where he'd often spend time taking photographs of the landscape and, well, picking asparagus.

Johnny

Beads of sweat formed at the top of Johnny's temples as he and his team stood behind the panoramic glass, watching the smoke rise in the distance.

"It's OK, guys, the heat is probably from the fire happening close by. Just open the windows and try to get back to work."

Ten minutes. Fifteen. Twenty. The cloud billowed higher in the air, and still no firefighters. Johnny unlocked his phone and started filming.

"It's been nearly half an hour since the fire started and nobody's showed up to the scene..."

Crackles of light flickered out of the smoke.

Against all logic, Johnny left the office to get a closer look. As he neared the blazing hangar, a mushroom cloud formed before him. Johnny stood motionless, watching it expand.

"Johnny, hide!" a voice cried out.

Just as he turned his back, a condensation cloud ripped through the atmosphere, flattening everything in its radius and throwing Johnny two meters away and into a wall.

Hassan

The sun set behind a stone house, its rays piercing Hassan's gaze as he walked back home. An abandoned football lingered across the street. Passing through the narrow roads of his village, Hassan failed to notice the empty chairs outside the village mini market and the unattended *shishas* by the sides of the street.

When he approached his home, the silence of his neighborhood finally broke. TVs in neighboring houses were all blaring loud news broadcasts. The closer he got to his house, the louder it got. Hassan leaned in, hoping to catch a glimpse of what happened, but only managed to make out a few words: "Beirut." "Firefighters." "Fire still blazing."

Johnny

Johnny woke to the sight of a red-orange cloud veiling the sunset he'd gotten so used to seeing every day at work. Muffled screams cut through the blaring alarms. Johnny looked at the sky in search of the condensation cloud he'd seen earlier, as if seeing it again would confirm what happened was real.

The straighter he stood, the deeper the glass dug into his back. Bleeding heavily, he remembered what he had learned from films, using his shirt as a makeshift tourniquet and tying it around his torso. Only fiction could have prepared him for this night.

He looked at his office, where the very same glass he had stood behind minutes ago was now shattered just a few inches away from his feet. Though his instinct told him to get medical care, he couldn't leave his team. Luckily, none of them were nearly as injured as he was.

Johnny and his team walked past the damaged silo as firefighters struggled to put out the flames that burned their way through the port and rescue
teams raced through the wreckage, yelling to one another and pulling corpses
out from the rubble. They saw an old man collapsed on a chair, his face ailing
and confused, his blood spilling out and mixing with the blood of those who
had already died and those taking their final breaths.

A woman with an exposed wound on her forehead ran towards Johnny:
"*Ahlak bel jabal.* Since your parents are away, I came to check on you." It was
his aunt.

When you happen to be in the center of catastrophe, you believe you're
its first and only target. Up until then, Johnny had forgotten all about family
members living in the area.

After securing a ride for his aunt, Johnny headed home. He walked
through the hole where his door used to be. The explosion blasted it off its
hinges and propelled it into the living room, where it lay with the shattered
remains of the white French doors of his balcony. The once ceiling-high cactus
had fallen and was wounded with glass, just like the wooden coffee table, the
beige sofa, the television, the laptop. Just like Johnny.

As he made his way back through Mar Mikhael, a motorcycle sped up
and slid next to him.

"Take me to the hospital," said Johnny. "I'm injured." His colleague, Naji,
did just that.

GeitawiHospital was blown to bits. So was Roum.

Making their way to yet another hospital, Naji's motorcycle ran out of
gas. Johnny was once again bleeding on the side of the road while trying to
hitch a ride to a hospital. A kind stranger finally drove them both to Hotel
Dieu.

Johnny bent over a stool in the hospital's waiting room while two doctors
examined his wounds.

"You have shards of glass in your back. One of them is as big as your
index finger. We're going to remove the biggest one and suture you up, but we
won't be giving you any anesthesia. We'd rather save it for more critical cases."

Johnny bit into his shirt as he fixed his eyes on the man sprawled out on
the reception counter, screaming. His attention was on the swarm of bodies

pushing their way into the emergency room. Women, children, domestic workers, laborers, and businessmen all made equal in one single blow.

"Most of them won't make it," he thought, "but we won't hear about them. Only those that died on impact will be respected enough to be counted among the dead in the official reports."

As Johnny made his way out of the hospital, he saw one of Lebanon's politicians and his security detail. "I'm half-dead. I might as well pull a jihad," he thought before screaming, "You're the last person I want to see right now!"

Naji pulled Johnny out the door where a news station had set up a live broadcast. Johnny didn't hesitate. Just as the reporter handed him the microphone Johnny yelled, "*Akeed hek baddo yseer* when we continue to let corrupted politicians *tehkom el-balad*. None of them care what's happening to the people. *Kiss ekht hek solta. Kiss ekht hek hokom.* Fuck them. This is all their fault."

Johnny and his colleague went back to his office to look for his phone. He runs into another one of his colleagues, who has a little boy quietly standing by his side.

"*Kiss ekht hal dawleh shou 'emlo fina…*"

"Johnny…"

"*Kiss ekht hek siyesiye.* These corrupt assholes fucked the country! *Neko ekht al-balad …*"

"Johnny. Stop. My sister died in the explosion. This is her son."

Johnny apologized and left. He went to a hospital in Jounieh, where they sutured the rest of his wounds. Lying in the hospital bed, Johnny opened Facebook and asked if anyone had a room or a spare bed. He, along with a couple of friends, ended up spending the night at Jean Marc's in Hamra, but they didn't sleep.

Hassan

Neither did Hassan.

With each toss and turn, a large gray cloud swirled in his memory. Two screens. His mother plastered in front of one, his father on the other. Two screens, three, four hundred thousand, a million. Some were shattered. Some were still brand-new, flickering in dark rooms, a choir dispersed all around the country, wailing in unison. Beirut: with her twentieth- century skyscrapers and nineteenth-century walk-ups, now flattened by 2,750 tons of ammonium nitrate.

Hassan sat up.

"I can't stay here."

After hitching a ride to a nearby village, Hassan climbed into a cramped van for Saida. Hassan stood on the side of a busy road waiting for the *jahesh el-dawleh* bus. He threw his bag into the van to Naameh and got in. He didn't look at anyone. He didn't talk to anyone. The Lebanese had a flare for theorizing in the wake of tragedy before getting all the facts, and Hassan had no patience for it.

"A hundred and thirty bodies found so far."

"New footage of the explosion shows the first blast."

"Fee ehtimel tkoun darbeh israeliyyeh. It may be an Israeli attack.*"*

"Yi lek l-mestashfayet—a woman gave birth in the dark. Doctors at Roum Hospital had to use cellphone lights for the delivery."

Each time the bus stopped, Hassan feared the information the new passenger's phone would bring.

Hassan puffed on his cigarette. The forty-five-minute drive ended up taking an hour and a half. The closer he got to his destination, the harder his heart pounded. Although he knew his house was damaged, he hadn't the faintest idea of what to expect.

From Cola, Hassan took a cab to Khandaq al-Ghamiq, where he grew up.

He walked into his doorless house, threw his bag on the sofa, and walked back out. Building after building looked the same: gates dislodged, house doors flung open, windows blown apart. Glass, glass, glass.

From Khandaq, Hassan walked to Saifi Village. Cafes, gift shops, restaurants, pubs all blown into holes, graves for the memories of the life once lived there. It wasn't the worst of it.

When he saw the blown-up balcony of one of the neighborhood's charming old buildings, he sat on the pavement and wept.

Johnny

Day-to-day survival requires logistical skill. Paperwork, budgets, and meetings require calculation and decision-making. But what about surviving the apocalypse? Why cater to the demands of daily existence when all rent paid is lost? When all plans are delayed? When all of one's reality is at the mercy of a flame ignited deep in the corners of a shipment container at a port that brought in more debt than it could cover? Such a catastrophe has no room in the logistical lives of a people already hungry.

All that is left is feeling, and Johnny felt a lot. Sleepless, Johnny put his shoes on and headed out.

A devastating night's silence was broken by the requirements of a new day. The unforgiving sun and the crowded roads betrayed the disaster that took place just over twelve hours ago. Life always continued, leaving little time for grief.

Johnny headed back to Mar Mikhael, his now homeless home. He stomped harder as he passed the police-mandated roadblock at the entrance to Gemmayze. It was 8 AM and people had already taken to cleaning up.

Johnny could've gone to the apartment his friend lent him in Badaro and rested, but the stitches burning his back, the smashed cars, the stench of nitrogen dioxide all lead him back to the *thawra*.

The revolutionary protests that had dwindled due to COVID roared back again. Crowds of people swarmed through Martyrs' Square carrying makeshift nooses, demanding the penalization of the governmental parties responsible for the displacement of nearly 300,000 people.

Johnny almost fell as the crowd pushed against him to escape the tear gas shot by the gendarmerie. It wasn't the first time he'd been in danger of getting hurt at the protests. Long before the explosion, before COVID, before the dollar rate skyrocketed, Johnny was chanting at the protests when a group of militiamen from the neighboring Khandaq buzzed through the people on their scooters, terrorizing everyone with their bats. Sectarian leaders had no shame in using such tactics against the people. Johnny was beaten up.

Hassan

Hassan collected himself and walked towards Electricite du Liban. Young men and women carrying brooms swept the debris and rubble to controlled piles by the side of the road. He marveled at the banged-up cars, the broken vitrines, and the dirty plush toys on the ground. He couldn't stay long; his girlfriend was waiting at her house in Ain el-Mreisseh.

Amid the shattered glass and fallen shelves of her seaside apartment,

Hassan and his girlfriend thought up ways to help those who need it. They managed to secure fifty sandwiches a day from a restaurant they knew and would go to Gemmayze, Mar Mikhael, and Saifi to hand out food to the people cleaning the debris. The sight of the old and young banding together to clean up their city reawakened a sense of hope in Hassan, a hope taken only moments later when he saw policemen filming themselves pretending to clean out glass from their headquarters, taking credit for the people's hard work.

It only dawned on Hassan that it had been a week since he visited Khandaq al Ghamiq when he returned. While Gemmayze and Mar Mikhael were getting cleaner and cleaner, not much had changed in his neighborhood. A friend approached him as he walked around.

"Where are the NGOs, the news channels? *Wayn al thawra*? Where are the revolutionaries?"

"Nobody came around to help?"

"My house is still shattered and my arm is cut."

"Let the party you so blindly follow take care of you."

Hassan passed through the street separating the mosque and the church he'd spent his childhood around, the same street that had instilled in him a hope for a united Lebanon and made him halt his immigration process so he could partake in the *thawra*.

"Khandaq al-Ghamiq and Mar Mikhael's borders are imaginary. What makes them real are the people in power."

When Hassan returned to his girlfriend's place, he sat on the bed and wrote a Facebook post in response to an image of a man covering his head amid the debris in Khandaq al-Ghamiq below an orange cloud with a red headline: "Khandaq al-Ghamiq is also in the heart of Beirut." Hassan's post read:

> I'm from Khandaq al-Ghamiq and I've been participating in the protests since they first started on October Seventeenth. I also went to Gemmayze, Karantina, and Mar Mikhael to help as much as possible. I did that with nothing but a pure sense of nationalism and love, without taking selfies or asking for any credit. Today's the eighth day since the tragedy that has befallen the Beirut Port, and I have two questions. One for the media and one for NGOs:

Where are the charities and NGOs that are supposed to be clearing out the mess and helping the wounded?

Where is the media that's supposed to be reporting the damages in Khandaq al-Ghamiq?

Khandaq al-Ghamiq is a street adjacent to Monot Street and has suffered the same damages. Khandaq al-Ghamiq is a nice street, and is home to many historical buildings. Khandaq al-Ghamiq has been hurt by the disaster that took place, the neglect of everyone else, as well as by its very own people.

All night Hassan's phone beeped. 366 shares, 57 comments:

You are our brothers but I wish you people knew the difference between those fighting for your rights and those coming to take away your weapons.

When the young, capable men of Khandaq al-Ghamiq are doing their best to strip people of their dignities and cause mayhem, they are not owed any empathy or consideration. Let those brainwashing them take care of them.

The problem is that some people tried and were kicked out of the area. It's the fault of the leading political party in Khandaq who are giving orders and preventing people from helping because it doesn't suit their agenda.

The problem is that the people of Khandaq al-Ghamiq have attacked protestors many times and burnt their tents. Had they joined forces with the protestors, we could've gotten rid of the entire class of people that has led to the situation in the country being this bad. The image they portrayed to people is that Khandaq al-Ghamiq is an area that's dangerous and closed-off from the rest.

Amid all the comments, only one was worthy of a response, one whose simplicity defied all opinion and pretense:

Can you meet us and let us in?

From Mar Mikhael to Khandaq al-Ghamiq

Mar Mikhael and Khandaq al-Ghamiq are only a five-minute drive apart, but for his whole life Johnny had heeded the warnings of those around him: Do not go to Khandaq al-Ghamiq—it's dangerous. They'll beat you up if you're not from there. The whole area is run by a militia, go at your own risk.

As the image of the burning silo replayed in his mind, Johnny couldn't stop thinking, "For decades our neighborhoods have been separated by barricades of fear so the reigning political elite could continue to benefit from our division. No more."

When Hassan responded, Johnny's excitement grew. After setting up a meeting two days later, Johnny created a Facebook post of his own:

Dear Friends,

I posted yesterday a call to go help the Khandaq al-Ghamiq following a call by someone that Khandaq is part of Beirut as well, and after a long day today, I just checked my messages and was looking to hear from one person and to my luck Hass Merhi got back to me (the person behind the post yesterday), I asked him about your worries if we go there if we will be beaten, requested to leave. And he said as I always thought, that we are WELCOMED.

I asked him that I will be coming with a bunch of people to CLEAN but he said it is cleaned already.

What is missing there is food, basic support, and medicine.

3 NGO have been present there but people are poor, people need food, people need meds.

So if you are up still to join me and go help there, let us bring FOOD, bring MED, and keep politics away! We are all Lebanese and that's what matters.

Who's in?

Meeting point 1:00 PM at Paul, Gemmayze.

If you are part of an NGO and you can provide food, join please.

NGOS PLEASE JOIN US.

Johnny's post received loads of attention, but out of the eighty-six people who liked his status, only fourteen showed up, nine of whom were women.

As Johnny and his friends walked past the green flags decorating Khandaq, a man clad in black wearing a baseball cap and leather messenger bag approached them. Johnny looked him in the eye. It was hard to tell whether this stranger in a mask was Hassan or somebody coming to question their purpose for being there. But before he could make up his mind, the man spoke.

"Hi everyone, I'm Hassan. Thank you for coming. I really appreciated your response to my post."

Johnny smiled.

"We're all brothers here. I'm only sorry we couldn't bring more people, but you know how us Lebanese are."

Hassan laughed. Neither he nor Johnny knew what to expect when they met. In many ways they were similar, both young, strong, and open.

"How can we help?"

Johnny and his friends followed Hassan into a beaten-up grocery store, where they bought fruits, water, canned goods and whatever meat they could afford. They then went into a pharmacy and bought an assortment of meds. They gathered on the side of the street, under the scorching August sun, rationing goods into separate plastic bags. Johnny stood in front of an old building posing for a photo, his body bent, his hand up, smiling like a child who'd just received the toy he'd been pining for.

Hassan led them deep into the trenches. Little, worn buildings, all stacked next to one another, each with a tent draping its entrance. Hassan, Johnny, and the rest of the group climbed the stairs of each building and knocked on doors handing out their donations.

The residents of Khandaq al-Ghamiq had grown accustomed to their own invisibility. Explosion or not, they'd long been left behind, defined solely by the political power reigning over their area and seen as traitors to a unified Lebanon—their resources scarce, their doors only knocked on during elections. But when Johnny and Hassan showed up at their doorsteps, they always greeted them with a smile or a glass of juice.

As they entered another building, a man on a scooter approached Hassan.

"Who are these people? What are they doing here in our neighborhood?"

"These are the people I told you about. They're here to help out."

"*La'*. You never told me about anyone."

Hassan wiped the sweat from his forehead as he pondered his next move. There were people with him, people who dared come help despite the potential risks. If he started a fight, he would be giving truth to every stereotype about the area. If he didn't confront the situation, he risked letting the party take credit for the donations. Hassan looked at his friends, then looked back at the party member. With a stiff upper lip, he reiterated what he'd told him.

"Yes. I did."

"*Tayyeb*, I'll let it slide this time. *Bas mnerja' mnehke ba'dan.* We'll talk about this later."

If there was ever a time Hassan felt sucker punched in the heart, this was it. His mind had been set on giving Johnny and his friends a positive experience in Khandaq, and yet despite all of his efforts and all of Johnny's, despite the crises the nation had suffered at the hands of the ruling class, despite the hyperinflation, the unemployment, the pandemic, the explosion, despite all the young people brutalized, detained, and prosecuted throughout the country for daring to come together and demand a better future, many still chose hate.

Hassan turned to Johnny and smiled.

"*Ahla w sahla fik. El mant'a mante'tak.* Our home is your home."

Written by Lynn El Amine
Story contributed by Hassan Merhi and Johnny Assaf

Beyond the Rubble

Note: Pseudonyms have been used throughout this story.

Having stories to tell doesn't always mean wanting to tell them.

After the 2006 war, all of that changed. Witnessing the ordeal of the displaced and the suffering of those who experienced the war firsthand had a lasting effect on me, even as a volunteer. Since 2006, telling my stories has been a way to keep memories alive, so that the suffering is not forgotten.

I also tell my stories for Lebanon. It is true that something dies inside me every time I experience tragedy through my work. Throughout the years, however, this has strengthened the bond I have with this land. My sense of belonging has deepened and has compelled me to continue serving, because this is my second home. The purpose of being a civil defense volunteer is to serve anyone in need and to fulfill a humanitarian mission, period. There is nothing that hurts me more than to not be able to heed that call because of who I am.

Today, this is why I have a story to tell.

Nothing can ever prepare you for something like August 4th. Even if you have what it takes, you pray to never have to face such tragedy.

It was hot that day, and my children were playing around in a makeshift pool, splashing water onto every corner of the terrace.

6:07 PM. felt like an earthquake.

Given the distance between Sabra and the Beirut port, we must have felt around 30 to 40 percent of the strength of the explosion. I ran up to the roof right away to make sure my family and children were safe. The thick white and crimson smoke looked unlike anything I had ever seen and seemed to have taken everything in its path. When something like this happens, we usually assume it's an Israeli strike or a targeted assassination. It never occurred to me that it would involve something ablaze in the port.

Less than five minutes later, I had already made my way to the entrance of Makassed Hospital along with a couple of other volunteers from the Shatila camp. We jumped in the first ambulance we found headed for Achrafieh. I knew I had to be there.

Being a Palestinian civil defense volunteer means heeding the call of duty wherever it may be, even if it is beyond the perimeter of the Palestinian camps that fall within our jurisdiction. Throughout the years, we have been on the ground together with our Lebanese counterparts to fulfill our humanitarian mission, from the suicide attack in Burj el-Barajneh and the Fassouh building collapse to the Ringo factory fire in Saida. Politics, as you can imagine, has always gotten in the way of us working on the ground.

Achrafieh was horror incarnate. Bloodied victims, dazed survivors, all terrified, enraged, and confused. Some were sobbing in silence, while others cried out loud. Either way, there was little that could be heard over the continuous soundtrack of ambulance sirens and the incessant smashing of broken glass that now paved the streets.

We didn't know where we were heading when we were hailed down to rescue a man trapped under the collapsed facade of a supermarket. Traffic was at a standstill on every main and side street, and it took us twice the time to reach our first operation. The Bangladeshi man trapped in the rubble, whose name I never knew, succumbed to his injuries before we made it. I cannot forget him, a foreign worker in a foreign land, alone, perhaps without any family nearby or anyone to ask after him.

Our ambulance was crammed with the wounded we accumulated on our way, as hospitals were over and above capacity. We finally found an ER that could take the injured. The scene was horrible. Bodies and blood everywhere. I didn't know what to make of all the chaos. Our small team of volunteers started assisting with triage and logistics. The Palestinian Civil Defense had already set up an operations room in the Burj el-Barajneh camp, coordinating support with the Palestinian Red Crescent. The camp's Haifa Hospital had also opened its doors to receive the injured, as hundreds of victims rushed to find any hospital beyond Beirut for immediate care. Our priority was to help as many people in danger and in pain as we could. We helped anyone we encountered in need. I must have helped around a hundred people that day. Nothing else was more important.

We returned to base after two hours and another group from our team headed to Achrafieh. Once on the ground, they were approached by our Lebanese counterparts who needed support with a specific rescue mission. A building had collapsed in the vicinity of the St. George Hospital and two possible survivors were trapped under the rubble. Their situation was critical. With the little equipment they had on hand, our team headed straight to the site.

Our biggest rescue mission was about to begin.

"I'm here, I'm here. I need oxygen," were the first words they heard from Ziad, trapped three floors beneath the rubble and barely visible. Helen, an Ethiopian woman underneath one floor, was sobbing. Thankfully, the team could see exactly where she was.

I headed back to Achrafieh with my colleague Bilal. We were stopped by law enforcement guarding a nearby street on our first attempt to reach the building.

"You cannot go past this line."

"I am Hussein Dimasi. I am with the Palestinian Civil Defense. This is my colleague Bilal..." I began, already frustrated at how long I knew this would take.

"I cannot let you pass."

"Our volunteers are already inside leading a rescue operation near St. George."

"I'm sorry. I cannot let you pass."

"The Lebanese Civil Defense asked us to lead this operation. My colleagues are already on the ground."

"You cannot pass."

I turned and decided to head back to our base, sadly accustomed to such behavior. As we neared the outskirts of Achrafieh, someone from another law enforcement branch called and assured me that we would be allowed entry.

The Palestinian Civil Defense was bestowed full responsibility for this operation and I was personally in charge. We needed all the support we could get. Lebanese law enforcement and our Lebanese civil defense counterparts, from a variety of different regiments, were all on hand. Specialized equipment from one of our own regiments also soon arrived. Hours after we started, a team of retired Lebanese army soldiers dressed in black gear marched to the site. Their dramatic entrance was anything but reassuring, and I immediately prepared myself for yet another confrontation. When they found me, they simply offered their help to ensure a successful mission.

We began by clearing the rubble in order to ease the rescue of Helen and Ziad and to protect everyone on site.

At first, we were unable to see or hear Ziad very clearly. Access and ability to communicate with him improved when we decided to open a hole in the wall of an adjacent building so we could see him clearly, as if he was sitting right next to us. We were also able to provide him with oxygen. He was under an unimaginable amount of pressure, knowing sudden death was a possibility, but I sensed another type of anxiety when he opened his eyes. I am certain he realized who we were from the badges on our vests and our accents. I could feel it. His defensiveness gave it away somehow.

Such responses to our presence are not new or unfamiliar. Take the 2019 Chouf wildfires. There was no time to coordinate. It was a race against time. Given the nature of the disaster and the imminent danger it posed to people's lives and homes, we got to the scene as fast as we could, even before our Lebanese counterparts. The astonishment on the faces of the locals was clear once they realized who we were. We could sense the fear in their eyes. The badges of our Ain El Helwe colleagues didn't work in our favor either, considering the camp's reputation. A local municipal patrol escorted us at all times, until the locals finally realized we were only there to help. We provided a humanitarian service, and the locals eventually reciprocated with humanity and helped us help them.

We needed Ziad to remain as calm as possible. As in any other rescue operation, we kept speaking throughout the ordeal, keeping him focused on our progress to distract him from the reality of his perilous circumstances. I also wanted to reassure him that we were there to get him out safely. Had he the choice, he probably would have preferred to be rescued by someone else. I can't tell for sure. Regardless, we did what we had to do for him. We were his only hope of getting out, and we would have done anything in our power to make that happen. "Please don't leave me," I heard him say. We never would have.

Whenever I think about that dreadful Tuesday evening, I always remember the darkness. Dark streets and endless commotion. Flickering streetlights and hazy flashlights occasionally illuminating the dust that filled the air and the rubble that continued to pile up all around us. It was August, and the humidity mixed with the debris made it difficult to breathe. The air also seemed heavier than usual. Whenever I left the site for a breath of air, I imagined what it was like elsewhere around ground zero, what other rescue operations were facing, how much worse things could be.

The rescue work was mostly done after midnight. Helen was freed at around 4 AM. The sun had already risen by the time we pulled Ziad out. Volunteers and neighbors gathered around and, despite the surrounding tragedy, burst into applause at the sight of the stretcher. At that moment, the smiles and tears of joy did not seem out of place.

In the days following the blast, we spoke to every official we could reach to offer our help. We were ready to do anything that was needed—reconstruction, repairs, assessments, search and rescue, anything to help our Lebanese counterparts and the Lebanese army. Over and over again, we were refused. Public officials told us that delicate nature of the situation and the location of the disaster meant our involvement would be limited. The purely humanitarian nature of our work wasn't enough. Still, we continued to help by organizing blood drives in the Badawi and Ain El Helwe camps.

Despite all obstacles, we managed to return to Achrafieh one last time when a fire broke out at the port less than a month after the blast. We worked with our Lebanese colleagues to put out fires in numerous warehouses, a delicate operation in which our female volunteers also joined. In the sheer enormity of the disaster, our work went virtually unnoticed.

Our Lebanese colleagues never miss us, though. They're always amazed and amused that we are everywhere! We have a great working relationship with them, our brothers in arms. They have taken a very courageous stance by working with us many times. Sadly, it doesn't happen often because they aren't the ultimate decision makers. When we are stopped from providing our services, it is usually by those who are far from what's happening on the ground and are not affected. When they stop us, our entire purpose and mission are brought into question. Few things hurt me more. I can only hope that our actions speak louder than words in defiance of those who stand in the way of what we do.

People have the right to think whatever they want, but nobody has the right to categorize me based on my national, religious, or political views. I know many Palestinians who hold many inaccurate, stereotypical views about the Lebanese from the war. We can't deny that the historical relationship between our people is complicated, but this doesn't mean we have to carry it on from generation to generation.

You know, I am partly Lebanese. Half of my mother's family is from the South. Identity is a complicated thing, but my humanitarian mission is not, nor should it be. As Palestinian Civil Defense volunteers, our role is humanitarian and humanitarian alone. We provide a service and ask for nothing in return. I only want to be treated like a person, who happens to be Palestinian, fulfilling his humanitarian duty.

August 4th was the most difficult and challenging experience of my civil defense life. Giving up was never an option. Tarek, Ziad's brother, did not survive the blast. But despite the pain of such loss, our efforts were acknowledged.

"Had it not been for you, I would not have survived," Ziad said in a message to my team, sent from the hospital just days after his rescue.

We want nothing for the missions we perform. We simply do what we, as Civil Defense volunteers, are meant to do. Although Ziad's rescue was like no other, I don't expect to see him again. We helped many people that day, and for me, once my service is done, I move on to the next mission.

I do what I have to do. It's truly as simple as that.

But, if I were to see Ziad again, I dream that it would be in my hometown, Jaffa, in my beloved but still occupied Palestine. We would walk around the old town. I would take Ziad to the Church of the Nativity in Bethlehem and then invite him to my house and reminisce, over coffee and oranges, about how we met under the rubble on that horrible Tuesday night. Yes, we would remember what happened and hope that it never happens again.

Written by Marina Chamma
Story contributed by Hussein Dimasi

Conversations with Ammo Samir

*H*ayate? *Shou baddeh illek? What can I tell you? My life* has always been a struggle, but I've kept it to myself. I never wanted anything from anyone. I never wanted to need anyone. I don't want to be a burden.

I've lived in this neighborhood in Geitawi, on this street, all my life. I was born here and have been here for the past sixty-eight years. I didn't get the chance to go to university. I really wanted to, but I had to serve in the army for a year first. When my service was over, the civil war had started and that was that.

You could say that the most significant job I had was installing satellite dishes. You know the dish, it gives a lot of channels, but sometimes they go out, so I would have to adjust the frequency and pick up payments. *Imagine, tkhayale.* I did that every day for seventeen years. Every single day for seventeen years, I would wake up at 5:30 AM, have my coffee, and go down to the ground floor where the office was. At 8 AM I would start walking. Up stairs, down stairs, up stairs, down stairs, sometimes 180 steps in one go, several times a day. I would walk ten kilometers every day and visit over 700 houses a month, a lot of them

with no elevators, mind you. I memorized every single one of those old buildings, the number of floors, the number of stairs in each ... *tkhayale*. Sometimes
I wouldn't get back until 9 PM.

Eventually, my legs gave way. I was worn out and in so much pain that I had
to leave my job. Since 2017, I have had no income, no social security, and *akeed*,
no pension. So, I'm stuck in my small apartment. I hardly ever leave. It's lonely,
you know. Miserable, really.

Before the explosion, all my days were exactly the same. I'd get up at around five
AM. Make coffee. Sit around, pass time on my chair, stare at the walls, maybe
watch a little TV. But it was always so boring so I'd turn it off, preferring the
silence. My lunch was simple, a bit of meat or potato, maybe I'd fry a couple of
eggs. Yes, I know how to cook, my *teta* taught me. But now, it's very difficult since
I can't stand on my feet for long. My back is severely rounded, see right here, I
can't even stand up straight, I'm always hunched forward and I have varicose
veins too. Even doing the dishes is hard. I remember a time when all I ate for six
months was tomato, cucumber, and bread. *Tkhayale.* Back when I was working, I
used to think that if I ever lost my job, everyone I knew could offer me something
small, like a bag of bread or a jar of olives, and it would sustain me for years. I
never heard from anyone.

After lunch, I'd nap and then I'd read anything I could get my hands on.
I have read so much over the years. I have two favorites. One is about how this
man, who despite losing an arm during the Algerian revolution, becomes an
artist, and the other is about a Shiite girl who leaves her village in the South to
discover the world. I'd completely lose track of time and, for a second, forget my
own reality. I read through all the books you and your friends brought me in just
a few weeks. Yes, in just a few weeks. I know you don't believe me, but I have all
the time in the world. These days, though, my eyes are bothering me. I have to
squint to read the words so I can't read that much anymore.

Anyway, dinner was usually a bite of fruit and then the evening news. Nothing
new there. Always the same problems and the same corrupt political faces.
What can I say, *this is Lebanon. Hayda Libnan.* After the news, I'd flick through
the channels looking for beautiful scenes from around the world, or I'd listen
to Umm Kulthum on the music channel. I'd stay up until 1 or 1:30, sleep, wake

up, and do it all over again. The same thing every day. I could have died and no one would have noticed, no one would have missed me. Why would they? I just wanted my time to be up. But after the explosion, everything changed. Everything changed for me after the explosion.

I had been sitting guard there for days, looking after the street. It was like war time, the same darkness and abandonment. But I stayed. Where would I go? To my brother's or sister's? No, no, I wouldn't be comfortable. I don't want to be a burden.

A young man came up to me in the street, *tkhayale*, a stranger, and you'll never believe what happened.

"Are you Samir?" he asked. So I said to him, "*Yee*, how do you know my name?" It turned out Mark had heard about me from the local church and came to offer me cash and food.

Then, just like that, my home was filled with strangers who became friends. Just like that, my home was suddenly filled with life. Lana, Rayan, Nour, and Tania came in and out throughout the day, clearing the rubble and doing whatever else they could. Tamara cleaned up my terrace and bought me a fan to deal with the suffocating heat. Majd, Jassem and George fixed the tile, the paint and the kitchen doors. Elie brought seven or eight guys to clear the glass, carry out the debris, and fix all the windows and doors.

Even a nun from Zahle came to see my home.

"Where are you sleeping?" she asked. I told her how large shards from the window had pierced the mattress but that it really didn't matter because I had been sleeping on a plastic chair for over a year and a half. With my back, the mattress was uncomfortable anyway. A few days later, a hospital bed was delivered. Can you believe that? The next morning, I woke up and realized it was the first time I had slept so comfortably in my entire life. *My entire life.*

You know what really hit me? The candles. All those candles flickering on the little cakes you brought out—the chocolate biscuit cake, strawberry tart, eclairs. Oh the joy! You can't imagine. I noticed you and Tamara sneak away, followed by some giggling and commotion in the kitchen. I was wondering what was going on when, suddenly, there you were, with the sweets and singing. And the candles! My home had never felt so bright. I don't know if you noticed, but tears welled up in my eyes. I was silent as you all sang to me, trying to process it all. It was enough that you all came despite the storm that trapped Mark in Zahle. I wasn't expecting it, I didn't want to be a bother. But you all insisted.

You know, I had forgotten what a birthday was until George came by the year before. He knocked on my door late one night, during another massive storm, with a chocolate cake and one big candle that burst like a firework. I hadn't had a birthday celebration in forty years. Yes, forty years. *Tkhayale.*

The BBC interviewed me down on the street, around the same time I had met Mark, and then MTV came up to my house to film the destruction. My sister saw me on TV and called.

I didn't often see my sister or my brother. They were both busy with their lives—my brother and his wife took care of a shop in Dekwaneh and were barely getting by, and my sister was busy with her family in Ain Zhalta. They'd call me once every couple of weeks and would send some food from time to time, but they couldn't do more than that. I don't blame them. Sometimes, a couple of friends I grew up with would come over and bring some food too. But mostly I was alone. Months would pass without seeing anyone, without a single phone call, but now this new phone George had brought me was ringing like mad.

It wasn't like the eighty-five daily work calls I would get, sometimes at five AM, to fix their receivers. No, this wasn't like that at all. This time people were calling to ask about me. *Me.* They wanted to know how I was doing, if I needed anything. *Tkhayale.*

People knew my name. They cared. They cared about me.

Around Christmastime, a Madame Haddad called me. She's Mark's aunt. She wanted to pass by with some treats. I told her I really didn't need anything, and that was the truth. All I need in life is water, Panadol, and Kleenex. If I don't have any of these, you've killed me, I'm done. But she insisted, and they came over for Christmas, and New Year's Eve too. They had brought the most delicious meat I have ever had. Of course, I didn't want to tell them so that they wouldn't feel obliged to bring me more. I never want to be a bother. Mark had also taken me to the supermarket, and we bought food to fill my fridge and some cheese and wine we enjoyed together. Up until that moment I hadn't left my home in years. Mark posted a photo of the two of us on Instagram and people saw it, I guess. A lot of people. *Tkhayleh*, imagine that.

That's how I met you, and here we are. This must have been, I don't know, just after New Year's? You wanted to hear my story for this book you're working on. You know, I thought to myself, why would she want to hear my story? But that's OK with me, I was happy to have someone to talk to.

I never imagined you would become like my daughter, my *bintee*. We talk about everything you and me, don't we? Your travels, work and family. About my health. We talk about Lebanon, of course, and this situation, don't get me started. I still can't believe how much I paid for a kilo of tomatoes. And Panadol! It has increased sixteen times, and at some point, they even didn't have any in the pharmacies. How are others even getting by? I know you still have hope for this country, but trust me, the only way anything will get better is for a foreign power to rule us, or a dictator to straighten things up. There's no other way.

You know, when you and Munir took me for a drive the other day, it was the first time in a very long time since I had left my neighborhood. Maybe twenty years. Looking out the car window, I realized just how much Beirut has changed. Hamra, I hadn't been there since before the war in 1975. I know it's just a ten-minute drive away, but nothing ever really took me there. My job was just around me: Geitawi, up to where Spinneys is, and back down to the Électricité du Liban area, and I never had the time to go any further. Weekends? What weekends? I never had a break. No, not even Sundays or holidays. There was always something. You know one time someone drove over in the middle of the night, begging me to adjust his TV while I was in my pajamas, *tkhayale*!

My favorite part of our day together by the sea, besides eating a hot cheese *man'oushe* off the *saj* after far too long, was playing *tawleh* with Munir. Remember how he first asked me if I knew how to play backgammon?

"Do I know how to play!? I hope you like to lose," I said to him, remember? We laughed about it.

It reminded me of this one time in the '70s, when I was with the army in Hasbayya. I had spent three of the best months of my life in that southern village. Nothing like the people there, so kind, generous, and welcoming. I was roaming around the village, looking for *bakdounes*, and I came across a family, I think it was either the Khodr or the Malaeb family, I can't remember. Anyway, they gave me the freshest batch of parsley from their garden and invited me in for coffee. I had gotten so consumed in a game of *tawleh* with one of the villagers, an older man named Abou Omar, apparently the *tawleh* king, that I lost track of time. I had no idea my unit was out looking for me. We played a couple of rounds. I won one, he won one. He couldn't believe it.

"No one in the entire region has ever been able to tie with me," that's exactly what he said. I remember it to this day. Little did he know that my father's uncle taught me how to play, and he was the true *tawleh king*, the backgammon champion of Lebanon!

Akh, I'll never forget that day.

It's been two years since the explosion. It's been a long time, so the phone calls, the visits, they've all dwindled. I understand. Life has to go on. I have gone back to my same old routine, but there are a few little changes throughout the day. I play card games on my new phone. *Likha* is my favorite. I listen to the voice notes you all send me, and scroll through Instagram and see the photos you all post. Oh, and TikTok! I spend hours watching those hilarious videos. They make me laugh so much! *Ma fikeh titkhayale. You have no idea.*

I do get a few visitors from time to time, like you of course. George also passed by the other day, and we had a little barbecue on the terrace. It was nice. Anyway, I don't blame anyone. My friends, yes, I can call them that now, they have lives that need living and I don't want to be a burden.

I know what you're thinking. I know you. Please don't be sad, but I can't, I can't lie to you. It is lonely again, but it is different, it is not the same as it was before. It is not like it was before the explosion.

So when you mentioned Munir's idea about holding *tawleh* tournaments on my terrace, I started to imagine how nice it would be to have people pass by a few times a week to play with me over a glass of arak. That one afternoon, when you came over and brought your friends to play a few rounds with me, that was really one of the most memorable times I had in my home. The first was my birthday.

So eh, I am alone again and, yes, life continues to be hard. But it is different. That's what I've been trying to tell you all along. If I die now, I know that people will miss me. I am sure of it.

Written by Zeina Saab
Story contributed by Samir Helou

What We Give

appy Birthday!"

"..."

"What's wrong? You seem off."

"I'm not sure ... I have a bad feeling. Something bad is about to happen."

Hassan is celebrating his twenty-first birthday at his home in the district of Akkar, in the northernmost part of Lebanon, when the explosion rips through Beirut's port and its surrounding neighborhoods.

"I have to go."

"No! It's not safe. Thank God you weren't there."

"I have to go."

"What will you do? What *can* you do? What if there is another one?"

"I am going."

"No! I won't let you!"

"I am going."

His mother, whose word he has never disobeyed until this moment, is dismayed. She wonders what drives her son into the line of fire, and if she will ever see him again. Hassan could stay safe in his own home and watch on a little screen, like many of his kin, the unraveling of a city. His city.

But he doesn't.

The car can go no further. Forum de Beyrouth, one of the city's most notable exhibition and concert halls, hosting the likes of Jose Carreras and Elton John, has all but fallen apart. Three hours after the explosion, the highway is partially obstructed and smoke fills the skies. Hassan and three friends from his revolution days set out towards the port on foot. They are no strangers to mayhem.

Green tanks struggle to redirect traffic. Red ambulances, their sirens wailing, struggle to carry the injured. Gray bodies struggle to move. Blank eyes struggle to find meaning. An injured man in his sixties struggles to reach his house. An ambulance is out of reach. The four young men lead him to safety.

About a year ago, when the Lebanese had feverishly risen to reclaim their nation, these four were among the first to answer the call. Millions of feet had stomped across the country demanding accountability. Millions of flags had fluttered, pumping life into the lifeless. Martyrs' Square in Beirut, the shining core of the revolution, the epicenter of hope and pain, had burned with the fire of hundreds of thousands of hearts yearning for freedom, screaming for justice. Heads wrapped in damp rags with cedar-tree flags for capes, they melted in a sea of a united Lebanon, impervious to religion, sect, or social status. They laughed, fought, danced, and cried with anonymous others, named only in common purpose. They defiantly rebuilt emblems of rebirth each time those were willfully destroyed. Together they had braved tear gas, police brutality, rubber bullets, and water hoses, forging a brotherhood in the trenches. They belonged, for months, to a dream far greater than themselves.

That dream is shattered. The square brims with shreds of cars, hotel facades, building panels, and furniture. Of metal, glass and human tissue. But mostly, lives that will never again be. A few steps into the residential neighborhoods of Mar Mikhael and Gemmayze, adjacent to the port, historic houses, shops, art galleries, and restaurants all disappeared into a painfully recognizable pile of dust and rubble. The same streets that had embraced Hassan when he flew the nest at only fifteen to make a life for himself in the capital now stand lifeless, pleading for resurrection. The four walk among the ruins. More dust. More rubble. A parade of bloodied mummies shuffling towards hospitals. They help where they can, all heart, with their young arms, until August 4th is no more. When the cold-blooded sun ushers in yet another beautiful summer morning, Hassan's journey unfolds.

Beirut is gasping for air. Her lungs poisoned with smoke, her breath muffled by horror, and her face shredded by glass. She stubbornly lives on, stumbling, supported by a thousand little brooms and a million big hearts.

Armed with nothing but a stick and a bag, together with people of all ages and from all walks of life, Hassan goes knocking door-to-door, steps into the cracks of severed lives and, irrevocably, into his own. Months of cleaning, renovation, construction work, search and rescue work, data collection work, and mental health support. Months of lifting, carrying, holding, and restoring broken souls that somehow still seem, at every moment, ready to break again. Months of sleeping outdoors in tents, sweating in heat, eating on streets, and talking in circles. Away from the family he knows, together with the family he makes. Penniless, jobless, and recurrently miscarrying his future.

"Exhaustion?"

"You forget exhaustion the minute someone you help smiles at you, or prays for you. It's all you need to keep going ..."

Working closely with three nonprofit organizations, including assisting one to set up a headquarters in Martyrs' Square, he feels more needs to be done. After buying a small drill, he embarks with a friend on a personal initiative to help repair damaged infrastructure in affected homes. He volunteers more of himself to blast victims. More of his sweat, more of his angst, more of his compassion.

He doesn't ask himself how much more can he give before he can't go any further, nor does he ponder if too much selflessness could erode the self. He doesn't wonder how much more external pressure he can bear before the internal structure collapses. Instead, he brushes off a raging pandemic, withstands an economic crisis in free fall, and ignores a political vacuum plunging the nation into poverty and lawlessness.

The breaking point, however, is easily reached. One too many horror stories, and each one becomes your own. Nightmares are common. Hassan startles with every humming helicopter he hears.

"You realize you are as much in need of mental health support as those you are providing it for, don't you?"

"..."

A new year is upon Beirut. Unemployment takes its toll. Making a living can no longer be ignored in place of making a life. Hassan finds a job renovating old homes in the neighborhood of Karantina, east of the port. All the same, he cannot fathom relinquishing his new-found world and all of its dwellers. He continues to volunteer part-time, determined to give back to the city that had adopted him when, at a very young age, he had decided to seek more. More than the fate he could have had, growing up in one of the most neglected parts of the country. More than a computer science degree aborted three semesters shy of graduation, courtesy of scanty internet connections and a lack of financial means. More independence, more open-mindedness, more freedom.

"Beirut is special to me. She gave me everything. I couldn't pay her back in a million years."

And yet he tries. He continues to wake up every day, reassembling fragments of lives forever fractured. Healing wounded souls still grappling to understand, let alone come to terms with grief and loss. Stone by stone, brick by brick, he continues to mend, patch, and fix. But when he enters an old heritage mansion all but ruined, he can't help but wonder. Can her walls ever again be filled? Can the divan ever again feel the warmth of a family gathered? Can the painting ever again stir the same feelings? Can the chandelier ever again light up a dance? Can the stories of a life of plenty and abundance, ever again be told?

The eldest of four siblings, he remembers growing up in a loving but modest household. Even as a child, Hassan quickly learned to fend for himself and help around the house. When his parents, his mother in particular, gave away basic necessities to neighbors in more dire need, he hadn't understood, until he did. Older, he recognized the power of giving and adopted it as a guiding principle. When he and his schoolmates had squabbled over toys, he was the first to let go.

"I've grown up with it. Maybe it's in my character. I'm not sure, but I know I have to give what I can."

Eight months later, he continues to give. When he reflects on his actions, he believes his experience has taught him valuable life lessons.

"My parents are very proud."

Perhaps altruism is Hassan's way to endure the unendurable and begin to comprehend the incomprehensible. Perhaps it is a coping mechanism that thwarts anxiety and depression by offering the illusion of control. Perhaps it is a blessing that has warded off the dangers of alienation by giving him a sense of purpose and community. Or perhaps it is, as he says, simply in his nature. What is certain is that very few people would do what he does, in the way he does it. He only now begins to recognize his singularity but is quick to brush off his fleeting discomfort.

"I would do it all over again, only better."

Written by Haya Hamade
Story contributed by Hassan Ali

Lost and Found

I was born and raised in the Ivory Coast. Almost everything I know about Lebanon is through its large expat community here, or whatever I experience when visiting family there every summer. That's about it really. I don't speak much Arabic and I am not very in touch with the culture. I've never even lived in Lebanon, but somehow I have such a strong connection to it. It's very weird. Lebanon is a huge part of my identity, but I still don't feel like I belong there.

I believe in social justice, and I've always been active for causes in the Ivory Coast and in London, where I pursued a law degree. I would spend hours upon hours in dizzying group meetings or raising placards in the rain before heading to the library to drown myself in towering piles of books and papers. I never worked on anything related to Lebanon before July 2020.

COVID-19 battered the global economy, but it impacted Lebanon especially hard since the country was already going through a financial crisis of its own. Migrant workers in the country, already living in such terrible conditions under the kafala system, basically modern slavery, were struggling to return to their homes, to their families and loved ones. I was born and raised in a country that welcomed me and made me feel so welcome, yet these women, from a handful of countries in Asia and Africa, had the complete opposite experience in Lebanon. Some were sleeping on the streets outside their embassies, waiting to be repatriated, while others had no embassy or active consulate to help them return. They were homeless, in the middle of a pandemic, in a foreign country. I posted something on Instagram to raise awareness about the issue and then set up a fundraiser with Beirut-based journalist Aline Deschamps, an activist in Australia and in Lebanon. I kept telling myself that we had to do everything in our power to get these women home.

And we did. There was a surge in donations. Celebrities like Gigi Hadid and Dua Lipa shared the post and it went viral. I still can't fathom it. By the end of the year, we were able to help forty stranded migrant workers get home safely and reunite with their families and loved ones. I was so proud of what we were able to do, but then I had a grim realization. If I, a twenty-one-year-old who barely knew what she was doing, was forced to take such a proactive role in resolving such a problem, then we were—we are—in really deep trouble. Surely, we had reached the bottom. Little did I know.

That morning, I graduated from law school, over Zoom of course. I felt proud and relieved to have earned my law degree after three years of endless readings and excruciating assignments. It definitely wasn't the celebratory ex-perience I imagined, but it was in 2020, the year of the absurd and unthinkable. To at least give myself a pat on the back, I went out to lunch with a good friend who helped me with the kafala fundraiser. In the middle of our conversation, I looked down at my phone and noticed my data was off. Once I turned it back on, I was barraged with notifications, the high-pitched tones ringing one after the other startled me. It was out of control and I was so confused. Even in hindsight, I can't remember how many messages I received from friends and relatives that day: "Are you OK?"

"Is your family OK?"

It hit me like a tidal wave, an emotional 180. Graduating had lifted a huge weight off my shoulders, but moments later I felt like I was about to get crushed. *What was it?* Bombs, attacks, and assassinations aren't all that novel in Lebanon. I recalled stories of the wars Lebanon went through, the political tensions that would spark violent skirmishes. *Surely it was one of those,* I thought. I sighed, and started scrolling on my phone to see what happened.

I saw the first video of the aftermath at the Beirut Souks and immediately realized how wrong I had been. All the windows of the high-end, glitzy shops were shattered, the structures destroyed. This ordinarily pristine bubble of comfort and privilege looked like the aftermath of years of war. My eyes widened and I started breathing heavily, the crushing weight pushing me down. I nearly dropped my phone when I found out the explosion came all the way from the Beirut port. I got goosebumps watching the same footage from different perspectives. No matter how many times I watched them, I couldn't believe what happened. That apocalyptic red plume of smoke mushrooming out of the warehouse, the screams, the destruction. For a moment I thought it was just a nightmare and I was going to wake up and get ready for my Zoom graduation. But no, this was real. This was very real and very different.

I rushed back home. I had no sense of time or place. It was like I was running in an empty void, but not actually moving. I arrived at 9 PM, or at least I think I did. It's all still a blur to me. I whizzed past my family huddled together, anxiously talking about the port explosion in the living room. I slammed the door to my room, sat on my chair, and started scrolling through my phone, still shaking uncontrollably.

Everyone was talking about it on social media, which was a lot like Beirut's streets. The horror, the fear, the confusion—we were all on the same page. For a moment I even thought I was there and not in Abidjan. I continued to scroll, struggling to stop shaking, losing count of the posts of pictures of missing loved ones, their names, a phone number, a cry for help. Television reporters read handwritten lists of patients from hospitals around Beirut, hoping viewers could identify them. There was clearly an urgent need to locate victims, but between the viral videos and the comments of shock and horror, posts about the missing were getting lost in the clutter. It was such a mess, such a mess. The information was all over the place and needed to be centralized, as accurate as possible, and constantly updated. *But how?*

I took a deep breath.

I scrolled across Ali Salloum's Instagram account, which I follow for his hilarious posts. But this time there was no comedy. He was reposting photos and information from different families. Some of my friends were doing the same thing. I was about to panic again, fearing this was adding to the unorganized mess, when I had my eureka moment. *Declutter! This is it!* I suddenly stopped shaking and focused. Setting up an Instagram account for missing victims would take minutes, and people could easily identify faces of friends and families.

I took a deep breath.

Time was of the essence.

"Lost People Beirut"? *No, that's a terrible name.* "Locate Victims Beirut." *OK, let's do it!* The page is up. I frantically messaged Salloum and asked him to direct people to the account.

I stared blankly at my phone, which at this point had become a detachable limb. I decided to take a breather, to put the phone down for a moment, but I couldn't. Those frantic, ear-piercing notifications started coming in again, ringing louder and louder. Hundreds of requests popped up. I read through them but could barely keep track. I got lost in all the photos and pleas for help. I couldn't comprehend what they were all going through—and I hope I will never have to—so I told myself to stay focused and start posting.

I couldn't get through the messages and post quick enough. Believe me, I couldn't. The explosion immediately impacted thousands of people, and there were equally thousands of requests to sift through. I called on my friends for help. All seven of us were on the account, repeating the same process like clockwork: read through the messages, vet the information, prepare the post, publish it. The more we posted, the more messages we got. We even had a few trolls distastefully try to prank us. On any other night, I'd have been outraged and given them a piece of my mind, but tonight was different.

In a matter of hours, Locate Victims Beirut hit 85,000 followers. Two days later, over 100,000. It became the centralized, most effective emergency response platform for the missing I imagined it could be, run by seven people with no experience whatsoever. Knowing this was bittersweet to say the least. I was proud of what my team and I were doing to serve people in need, but I couldn't help but be furious about the state's absence and negligence. Where was the Health Ministry in all this? How did the hope of so many people rest on some random Instagram account?

The first missing face I saw was Ralph Malahi, a twenty-three-year-old firefighter. I distinctly remember two photos of him: one in his firefighting gear, the other of him looking into the camera with a subtle smile. His cousin was on Twitter, and her call for help resonated with many. It really touched me. I received a lot of messages about him. He was only two years older than me and had his whole life ahead of him, but he died alongside at least nine other firefighters. I remember seeing pictures and videos of his funeral. His colleagues in uniform held his coffin, draped in the Lebanese flag, over their heads. At his church, his jacket was placed right by his coffin, "the martyr and hero" right by his name.

There was also twenty-three-year-old Joe Akiki who worked at the Beirut port. His family waited for a tormenting three days until Civil Defense first responders pulled his body out of the rubble near the destroyed silo. Just hours before, his mother said on TV that the family was hopeful they would find him. I cannot imagine what they felt. I just can't.

The stories of Akiki and Malahi hit me hard. I had a really difficult time accepting that they, and so many others, passed away. And for what? It was all just so cruel and so unfair.

Anyway, there was no time to think, and no time to let my emotions get the best of me. I needed to focus on the process I was locked into: read, vet, prepare, publish, repeat. But I suppose it was inevitable that I'd let my guard down.

Many of the people reaching out to us were children. Children! I remember this one request, and I swear to everything that I will never forget it, where a child reached out to me with information about his dad. He was twelve years old. Twelve years old, and I remember feeling so scared for him.

"Please, he's my dad. Please repost this quickly." My stomach churned and my heart sank. I was running on empty at this point. I stopped to comfort and assure him that we were doing everything we could. Unfortunately, we later found out that his father passed away. I still think of this child to this day. I really, really hope he didn't find out over social media. That would have been horrible.

News spread like wildfire and people were rampantly sharing whatever came out, commenting on the posts with updates, hopes, and prayers. We kept working throughout the night, and surprisingly we started to hear from international media. The *New York Times*, the *Washington Post*, and even *Vogue*, of all places, wrote about Locate Victims Beirut. I really couldn't comprehend what was happening, I just kept trying to read, vet, prepare, publish, read, vet, prepare, publish …

And then we crashed. Instagram shut us down, not once but twice. I had to contact customer service and convince them that we weren't a spam account. One of my teammates, Emma Sleiman, suggested we build a website that allowed people to submit information and photos of their missing loved ones through a portal, which would be a faster, more effective process for everyone. Emma was sixteen at the time. In fact, the whole volunteer team were teenagers. Akshit from India, just eighteen, built the website and database overnight. Muwaffak from Syria, who was studying in the Ivory Coast, built a database for first responders, municipalities, and hospitals, so we joined efforts and helped him populate his. They were all so incredible; an endless source of energy and hope.

After a few weeks, when requests for missing people stopped coming in, we expanded to take part in the wider relief effort. We fundraised to help families cover expenses for rent, medicine, and food. I mean, financially supporting victims of the blast and their families was crucial, especially since Lebanon was already going through such a terrible economic crisis.

One of our more miraculous moments was when Eleni, an Ethiopian domestic worker, was found. She was unidentified and in a coma after sustaining severe trauma to her head and leg. Karim Kattouf, an activist, used Locate Victims Beirut to find her. When she regained consciousness a month later, he set up a fundraiser so that she would not return home empty-handed. We managed to raise almost $6,000!

We also worked with a professor at the American University of Beirut who was helping with renovations in the Karantina neighborhood near the port, where many economically vulnerable communities live. Emma and I attended the Young Activist Summit, organized by the United Nations and Dev TV in December that year. We spoke about this incredible solidarity alongside other inspiring activists. To this day, I am still overwhelmed by everyone's generosity and kindness when I look at how much money we were able to raise. How people came together to support one another is still so unbelievable.

I mean, the explosion is still so unbelievable. You know, it took me seven months to even begin processing what had happened. Suddenly, a lot of thoughts that I had suppressed or ignored came flooding back, including exasperating questions about where I belonged in all of this. But you know what, I think it's quite Lebanese to feel you belong everywhere except in Lebanon. All the crises over the years have pushed and continue to push people away, creating diasporas worldwide that experience the same dilemma. While thousands, if not millions, of us spend lifetimes trying to figure out our relationship to Lebanon, many of us will try to "earn" our belonging by continuously trying to support its people. I guess *that* is what probably makes me truly Lebanese.

Written by Kareem Chehayeb
Story contributed by Zahraa Issa

Dearest Krystel

You don't know me, but I had to write to you.
If I put these thoughts out into the world,
down on paper
in words
seen and held
by the shaking hands
of those who have survived you
Maybe then
just maybe
they will float to you like a prayer
and you will know that you have touched
so many lives.
Still alive.
You'll know, I hope.
I hope you'll know.
I hope.
Still,
I hope.

Dear Krystel,

There were so many strangers that became your friends in that little neighborhood you called home, *call* home. You were, you are, you remain one of the good ones. They called you *moudira,* endearingly, because you took care of them all, *boss.* They still call you *moudira,* you know.

You never once made anyone feel *less-than,* never once made yourself *more-than,* never once regretted returning from abroad, never once questioned your faith in God, never once saw your own acts of kindness. You were, you are, you remain simply you. Existing, resisting, persisting.

Dear Krystel,

Moudira. A young man, a valet parking attendant, "*Moudira,*" he said. "I want to immigrate to Germany but it's all so complicated. The visa applications are not made for people like me, not *me.*" You weren't going to have that, not you, so you did what you thought any person would do. You helped and you wrote and you read and you helped and you applied on behalf of the young man in the neighborhood you called home, that calls you home, that remains your home. Because of you, he wasn't there that day.

Dear Krystel,

Your dad likes the green and fresh *foul* from your village, not from the store or from the local vegetable stands. No, he likes them from the land. So you drove all the way up there that one time, brought them all the way back, so that your dad could have an extra bit of joy, that day, that one day you drove all the way for no other reason except him. For the sake of bringing him joy, in the smallest bean of *foul,* on that day, that one day.

Making someone smile is worth all the effort, you used to say. You used to say, those are the true miracles.

Dear Krystel,

You had a special way with him, with Mario, and he loved you, Krystel, so much. *Moudira.* You met Mario from the church group. He became your family and you became his. You were his, are still his, will always be his. You would often go to that little house in Mar Mikhael, the neighborhood you called your own, the one that calls you home, that will always be your home. After work, you

180

would visit him and his *teta* with something they might need—some groceries, a smile, a *rakweh* of coffee shared on the balcony, a listening ear to hear *Teta* say, *God bless, we make ends meet*. One time you paid a bill for them that they never found out about, that one was by design. Those are the true miracles. Mario, he was only nine, his own mother having left him with his grandmother all those years ago. He was only nine, but he knew how special you were, you are, you will always be. He knew it the way a nine-year-old knows it, the way that an essay titled "My Hero Is…" shows it. Mario didn't hesitate. He knew who his hero was, who she is, who she will always be.

They were having trouble, that summer of 2020. The pandemic did a lot of damage but *God bless there are others worse off, others don't have you, others are worse off, God bless*. Mario needed a laptop because school was now online. He'd never had a laptop before and, anyway, they can't afford it. *How will the boy go to school? God will provide. God always does*. God and a village. It takes a village. But Beirut wasn't a village, you were. You were, you are, you will always be their village, their kin. Making someone smile is worth all the effort, that's what you used to say.

You left your work in the afternoon, you worked as a manager of a bank, and on that day, you planned to go to your parent's house just outside the city, but you were running late. You took Mario to the mall to pick up the laptop you had your eye on and you would spend some time setting it up and showing him how to use it. *Zoom. Zoom. Zoom*. He loved that sound, and now he was going to learn to use the program. But first, the escalator. He wanted to go up and down, to see if he could run backwards and catch it off guard. Every child has done that at least once, that thought must have crossed your mind. When you took Mario back home, you sat on the kitchen table and looked over at the couch in the living room. This is where Mario sleeps and often builds forts with the cushions. *Teta* was making coffee, and she placed it on the table as you opened the laptop, and patiently went through the basics of hardware, software, the internet, *zoom zoom zoom*. You tested the camera and microphone. Mario was having a great time. Mario then turns to you and asks you to be his mom. You look at *Teta*, *Teta* looks at you. Mario tells his grandmother, *you're my teta, so it's OK for Krystel to be my mom*. You knew how much the moment meant to him, but you also know how important the truth can be. It's the foundation of true love. You explain to him that you would love to be his best friend, and that you'll always be there for him. *Best friend.* He turned the words around in his mouth and loved the sound of them. *Best friend.*

Dear Krystel,

You walked away from their home that day. That day, you had no idea what was coming. Nobody did. It was a day like any other, except you were running late. You decided to stop by your apartment in Mar Mikhael, the neighborhood you call your own, the one that calls you home. You never really stayed there, but home is where your community is. The apartment was just an old family heirloom that you could use on a day like today, when you were running late. You called your mom. *Mario needed some help with his new laptop, I'll be late.* Your mom didn't mind. *You'll get here when you get here, we'll wait.* So you walked into the building, up the stairs, and put down your things. Moments later it became that day, that day, the day.

You were there, under the weight of the bookcase. You reached for your phone and dialed your father for help. He was on the ground, a first responder, stitching up the injured, carrying them to cars and motorcycles to get them to local hospitals. When he heard your voice he dropped everything to come to you. He did. He dropped everything and raced to you and when he arrived, he carried you and told you to please, just please, hang in there. He put you in an ambulance full of people and they wouldn't take anyone else, so he couldn't join you, and he had no idea which hospital you would end up in, and all that was left was prayer.

You made miracles happen, Krystel. But you are flesh and bones and blood. A body that could no longer hang on. You died on the way on that day. That day. The day.

The whole world, your whole world, the neighborhood that you called home—calls you home—wept. So did Mario. And his *teta.* And your parents (Your parents every single day). And your brothers. And your friends. And the valet parking attendant. And the staff at your local pub. And the whole world, your whole world wept.

Dear Krystel,

Moudira. Months later, after our whole world went down to the streets and swept and wept and helped and fed each other, and rebuilt and donated, after all that, Mario and *Teta* sat in their little home. *Teta* was making a *labneh* sandwich, and Mario had just finished school on his laptop. The doorbell rang. A washing machine had arrived. They always washed by hand, never the luxury of a machine. *Teta* was sure it was a mistake. The men told her it was an anonymous donation. *Teta* knew what that meant, and so did Mario. He said, *This is Krystel. She is my best friend. She's always there for me.*

You were, you are, you will always be.

Written by Nadia Tabbara
Story contributed by Dr. Nazih Maroun El Adm and Dalal Khadra El Adm

Afterword

After her tragic passing, Krystel's friends and family launched a charity foundation in her name. Her loved ones were certain that she would want to continue to help others through selfless deeds. The Krystel El Adm Foundation opened with the primary focus of helping children in Lebanon access education. Within a year of its creation, the foundation has already sponsored more than 2,000 students across Lebanon, paid tuition, and helped provide books and other school supplies across the country. For more information, please visit krysteleladmfoundation.org

From Rage to Change

M aya felt light-headed as soon as she hung up the phone.

Lynn, a fellow med student, was waiting for her in Sassine Square, along with Joe Nassar, a third-year, and Elias. Joe had a plan to run an independent list in the student council elections at the University of Saint Joseph medical school. Did Maya want to be involved? Could she come meet them now?

Sassine was about a kilometer away from her house. The late September afternoon was cool and breezy, so Maya decided to walk. As she put on her shoes, she thought about Joe. When the revolution began last October, they often crossed paths at the USJ encampment in downtown Beirut, where they were both regulars, but they didn't know each other well. As far as she knew, Joe's family home in Mar Mikhael, at walking distance from the port, was destroyed in the explosion, and they were still staying with family outside Beirut.

Maya thought back to August 4. The shattered glass. The horror, rage, disbelief. People searching for their family members. Phone lines barely working. Everywhere, blood. A fifth-year medical student, Maya immediately headed to the closest hospital and spent the entire night, into the next day, holding and comforting the injured while they waited for treatment in half-functioning medical facilities—amid an airborne viral pandemic to boot. In the weeks that followed, she supported wherever she could: cleaning debris, helping repair damaged houses, assisting the displaced and injured. She spent an entire afternoon helping an old man, who had lost his house, search in vain for his missing cat.

Over 200 dead, thousands injured, tens of thousands of homes destroyed and lives uprooted. Could it be that the government and political ruling class had done this from sheer criminal negligence yet would face no accountability? Were ordinary residents in Lebanon completely powerless to do anything about it?

Maya practically ran to Sassine, her mind buzzing with anger, despair, and possibilities. Lynn, Elias, and Joe were seated outside in a small park, talking enthusiastically. The late summer breeze and light smell of wild flowers gave a sudden sense of normalcy that Maya had largely forgotten.

Joe seemed more excited than she had seen him in months: "So great to see you. I have a plan!" He dove into his pitch immediately: The country may be run by generations of militia men, feudal lords, and war criminals, but the university didn't have to be. Independent slates had been making gains at other universities, and USJ elections were six weeks away.

"I propose we revive the independent student group campaign and run in the medical school elections. As it stands, our student government body is dominated by the Lebanese Forces and their allies, on the one hand, and the Free Patriotic Movement and their allies on the other. No independents ran last year, but I am certain that now, after the *thawra* and explosion, we can guarantee some seats out of the thirteen. We might not be able to change the country," Joe urged them, "but at least we can try to change our university."

The cruel genius of the Lebanese ruling system is that it maintains itself by controlling access to jobs, social services, permits, legal documents ... even access to visas and places at "good" elementary schools are regularly mediated through the various militia-parties. It is very difficult to get anything substantive done without passing through this favors system that produces and reproduces sectarian-based loyalties. Student elections at USJ and other universities function much in the same way. Practice medical exams, information on internships, opportunities for foreign study, and specializations are all mediated by the two main political parties. People vote for them, in part, for those opportunities, and odds are heavily against any kind of opposition.

Maya, Elias and Lynn doubted they could win, but Joe's voice was calm and assuring.

"We have to try. At the very least, we can make the political factions publicly defend why they should maintain control of what should be collective resources. At best, we might change a few minds."

They named their list Abyad—the color white—as an act of defiance against the parties' absurd appropriation of all colors of the spectrum.

Before October 2019, Maya channeled her commitment to social justice into her studies. Becoming a doctor would give her the tools needed to help others suffering or in need. When the *thawra* erupted, she began to connect the dots. As a doctor, how could she serve people in a country without a national public health infrastructure? What is health without regular running water, safe roads, and access to well-paid, secure jobs? Seeing thousands in the streets around her, fighting for a dignified life so that their families could live happily, that was what well-being looked like.

She became a regular at the protests, blocking roads and marching on Parliament. She met Joe at the USJ organizing tent. It was great to know she had someone to count on in the medical program, though their struggle was still focused on one common goal: to wipe out the entrenched, relentless Lebanese regime and all of its influence.

Joe came from a politically active family. His parents had participated in demonstrations in the 1990s around reconstruction, the fate of downtown Beirut, and support for trade unions. They didn't like any of the political parties. When the unexpectedly large protests broke out in 2019, Joe was delighted. Life in his family's two-bedroom flat had become increasingly exhausting. Because it was an old building without a generator, they were reliant on the neighborhood *ishtirak* mafia, which kept increasing prices as electricity cuts became more frequent. His parents struggled with the increasing cost of living, which included his medical school tuition and school fees for his younger siblings.

From October 17 onward, Joe hardly missed a day downtown. His medical studies became secondary to the goal of helping imagine and form a country in which health and wellness might be possible for all.

But the blast was different. To say that Joe's world turned upside down made light of the experience. His house was destroyed, his family displaced. Maybe it would be more accurate to say that time ceased to have meaning. Endless rubble and broken glass stood in for memories, disrupted lives. Joe joined the young and old together to clean their neighborhood, mourn the murdered, fix their homes—simply put their lives back together—in what became a form of collective struggle. For Joe, this wasn't enough.

A massive demonstration was called the Saturday after the blast. Joe arrived early to the smell of tear gas and sounds of enraged cheers. Something already felt different. As the day went on and more and more protesters arrived, tears of anger mixing with the noxious gas, the state police forces rapidly escalated their violent repression: more water cannons, more rubber bullets, more arrests. *How could they be so vicious? Didn't they also lose family in the explosion?* So many months, so many protests, and still the government was able to commit a crime of such magnitude with no consequence.

Something shifted inside Joe. He knew they had to change fronts.

Registering to run was surprisingly easy. Maya elected to run as treasurer, and Joe ran as president of the Abyad list. They sent an email informing the administration of their intention to participate in the elections and received a quick reply from the school: "Student elections are an important part of our educational mission and our country's practice of democracy." Joe almost burst out laughing. "Please submit your thirteen-person list of names."

As soon as Joe and Maya began telling their classmates of their plan to run, their list filled up with eager candidates, including friends and people they didn't know well.

Andrea signed on because she couldn't stand to hear the political parties' speeches at every university event any longer.

Karim felt like elections were mostly a symbolic exercise, but he agreed a victory would be important.

Nabih thought they might actually be able to make real change.

Abyad's first major step was to create a party platform, based on student needs. They began working systematically, adding points to their electoral plan based on their discussions with their peers. The platform planned to democratize access to information and opportunities that the political parties controlled and leveraged. If elected, Abyad promised to institute universal access to all past exams and relevant study materials and, true to their word, set about collecting them. They vowed to improve online classes that had become the norm during the pandemic, asking instructors to present interactive sessions on Zoom, rather than the often dull and confusing prerecorded lectures. They began researching opportunities for international internships and medical residencies—which most students didn't know how to access—and organized an online informational event. In coordination with the USJ Secular Club, they even started organized discussions about demystifying the national electoral process.

Soon, other students started seeking them out and reaching out to other students in their year, disseminating the platform and invitations to meetings. Through their growing list of contacts, they arranged meetings with the students in each of the medical school's promotions.

Throughout October, Maya's energy was so focused on the campaign that she nearly forgot she had to go to campus and sign paperwork for an internship. Almost all courses had gone online, and the organizing work was all-consuming. On a drizzling Tuesday, she gathered her ID card, multilayered masks, and some election posters and headed to campus.

The medical school was practically empty compared with pre-pandemic days, and the logistical meeting went quickly. On her way out of the main administrative hall, Maya paused and pulled out a poster and tape from her bag. As she began putting up the poster, a voice startled her from behind: "Abyad—all white. Pfft, couldn't they have been more creative with their colors?" Maya turned around to see a young man, wearing jeans and a plain green T-shirt. She didn't recognize him, but it was a big school.

"It's against the parties' appropriation of the color spectrum."

"Not very interesting. Anyhow, I hear they have no chance."

"Who did you hear that from?" she replied calmly.

The man paused, a smirk subtly spreading across his face. "Let's just say, I've heard it's not a great idea to run an opposition campaign in times of political crisis."

Maya's composure surprised her. "Let's just say, that's exactly when to run."

She turned her back to him and finished hanging the poster, taking deep breaths to control her racing heartbeat.

Truly, as the group's popularity and message spread, so did the opposition. Maya and Joe started hearing rumors of veiled threats. One student mentioned they'd overheard a small group of students listing the names of the candidates and their home addresses. But there was no proof, nothing they could take to the administration to show intimidation.

As the election date approached, news of independent victories at other student council elections across the country began to be announced: the Secular Club at the American University of Beirut won an unprecedented 85 of 101 seats; at the Lebanese American University, the independent student group won unanimously.

Their organizing list alone grew to a hundred members, with even more interested. Many people who had never been involved in politics were infuriated by the blast and the utter lack of accountability, and wanted to channel their energy into change—however small it might appear at first glance.

Joe and Maya's excitement grew. They kept close tabs on their progress, tallying their anticipated vote counts and campaigning for more. They would send out daily text messages to students highlighting the urgency of voting. With the elections two weeks away, they couldn't afford any missteps. They had come a long way in a little over a month, but this was the moment that counted the most, and they'd have to campaign harder than ever before ballot day. They couldn't lose momentum.

Maya was rarely able to find moments of pause between studying, classes, and the final campaign stretch. After a long study session preparing for a chemistry exam, she stole a little time on the balcony, taking in the evening air. It was a bit cool, a welcome break from the warm October weather. Yet it was also a reminder that winter might make the pandemic worse. She pulled her sweater robe in close around her and thought about her grandparents living alone outside Beirut. She was worried about them, as the COVID numbers continued to rise. She glanced at her phone on the table. She'd missed a call from Joe. It was 11 PM, and unlike him to call so late without texting first. Maya's first thought was that something bad had happened with his house—the reconstruction was going slowly—but then she remembered how blasé Joe had seemed yesterday about it, in contrast to his sheer excitement for the elections. Anyhow, it was late, she should have probably gone to sleep and called him in the morning, but something told her to check in.

Joe picked up quickly.

"Maya!" He sounded agitated.

"Is everything OK?"

"Maya, we won."

"What do you mean we won? The election is still two weeks away ..."

"We won! The Ouwwat and Aounniyes pulled out. I just got a congratulatory email from Student Affairs."

Maya nearly jumped from her seat. "We really won?"

"We won! We won the whole list! All thirteen of us!"

Maya almost couldn't believe it. In less than two months, they'd done the impossible.

As news of their victory settled in, Maya, Joe, and the expanded team set about putting their platform to work: improving online classes to favorable responses, centralizing access to educational resources, organizing various online discussions around student interest. A lecture by sexologist Dr. Sandrine Atallah drew a crowd of 150 students. The group expanded beyond its own territory and organized meetings with other independent student groups—the Secular Clubs at the Lebanese American University and the American University of Beirut—with whom they agreed to attend protests as a united front.

Abyad's apparently small victory has had important resonance so far, but Maya and Joe insist that they still have a lot to do. It's easy for people to abandon their allegiances from a place of anger, but now the real work begins: to grow their reach; to inspire more students to do the same in their own schools and universities, in their local municipalities and at their jobs; to create other forms of social support, sustenance, and flourishing that bypass the regime and all its manifestations. Maybe that is what justice really looks like: undermining the reach, control, and dominance of the ruling classes by building power together.

Written by Mary Jirmanus Saba
Story contributed by Maya Rammal and Joseph Nassar

THE WRITERS

AJ Naddaff
AJ Naddaff is a multimedia journalist and translator pursuing an MA in Arabic literature at the American University of Beirut. His work has appeared in the LARB, the Associated Press, *The Washington Post,* The Intercept, and *Columbia Journalism Review,* among other outlets. Follow him on Twitter @ajnaddaff.

Carmina Khairallah
Carmina Khairallah spent the first twenty-five years of her life in Beirut before moving to Paris in the summer of 2020. Throughout the years, her writing has taken her from concert reviews to spoken-word poetry. She has a BA in illustration and is currently training to become a tour guide. Find her on Behance: https://www.behance.net/CarminaK

Hala Srouji

Hala (Halo) Srouji earned a BA in journalism from the American University of Science and Technology in Beirut, Lebanon. She traversed several countries and career niches for two decades before returning to Lebanon in 2020. She was the corporate communications general manager at the Port of Salalah from 2012 to 2015. Hala has read her poetry at open-mic events in Beirut, Dubai, and New York, exploring issues of third-culture identity, feminism, and Arab history.

Haya Hamade

Haya Hamade is a freelance creative writer and translator, former pediatrician, and Harvard public health graduate. She has worked with prominent publishers, as well as individual and corporate clients in various fields from media to academia. She speaks five languages but will never understand extremism. Born and raised in Beirut, she has nonetheless chosen to set up permanent residence in Neverland. You can reach her at hayahamade@gmail.com

Jasmina Najjar

Author of *Beirut Knights, Being of the Cedars* and various journalistic articles, Jasmina Najjar is a conceptual copywriter, marketing consultant, and an academic. Raised in London, she currently resides in the UAE. She has a BA in English literature, an MA in literature, culture and modernity, and a postgraduate diploma in professional marketing. A bookworm, film fanatic, and art lover, she loves conducting research and learning new things.

Jenny Gustafsson

Jenny Gustafsson is a writer/journalist and photographer from Sweden, living in Beirut since 2009. She writes about various issues related to society, culture, development, migration, and politics. The topic closest to her heart is handicrafts and textile traditions, including embroidery and weaving. She works across the Middle East and parts of Asia and Africa, and contributes regularly to various international publications. Follow her on Instagram @jenperspective or visit her website at www.atjenny.com

Kareem Chehayeb

Kareem Chehayeb is a Lebanese journalist based in Beirut whose work often focuses on human rights, marginalized communities, economics, and politics. His work can be found on a handful of platforms, including Al Jazeera, Sky News, Middle East Eye, the *New York Times*, and the *Washington Post*. Instagram: @kareemchehayeb; Website: kareemchehayeb.me

Lynn El Amine

Lynn El Amine is a writer and artist. After finishing her MA in Creative Writing (ARU, Cambridge), she co-taught literature alongside Dr. Ziad Suidan and worked as a freelance writer. She currently teaches English communications courses at Haigazian University. When she isn't working or drawing, Lynn conducts writing experiments and logs their effects on the writing process as well as the overall outcome. Some of her work can be found in Turning Point's poetry anthology, *And we chose everything*. You can reach her at lynnelamine@gmail.com.

Marina Chamma

Marina Chamma is a Beirut-based political economist and author. Her first book, *And So We Drive On*, a collection of short stories inspired by Lebanon and life in Beirut, was published in July 2020. Follow her on Facebook and Twitter @eyeontheeast.

Mary Jirmanus Saba

Mary Jirmanus Saba is a filmmaker and geographer. Her feature debut, *A Feeling Greater Than Love* (2017 FIPRESCI Critics Prize Berlinale Forum), revisits the pivotal role of women in Lebanon's powerful 1970s labor and farmer movements. Her new collaborative works explore the intersections of labor politics, feminism, and finance capital, aspiring to imagine and create new political horizons.

Micha Tobia

Micha Tobia is an editor and a writer, currently based in the US. She is the co-founder and co-editor of Mashallah News, a storytelling platform about the Arab world and is the editorial manager at the Tahrir Institute for Middle East

Policy. Despite it all, Beirut's old buildings, purple jacarandas, sunsets, unexpected and hidden little gems, and its people are what she wants to remember of the city.

Nadia Tabbara

Nadia Tabbara is a writer/creator of film and television. She is currently based in Beirut and has produced three Lebanese TV series. She is also the author of *Harness Your Creativity*, a book detailing her decade-long research on the creative process, and an established creativity coach who shares her specific methodology with aspiring writers at FADE IN:, a writing hub she opened in 2014 in Beirut. Wherever she is, or whatever she's writing, you'll always find her with a cup of coffee by her side, creating worlds of fiction one word at a time.

Niamh Fleming-Farrell

Niamh Fleming-Farrell has lived in Beirut since 2009 (apart from an ill-advised stint in Dubai), where she has worked variously as an editor, a journalist, bookseller, and waitress. She is the co-founder of Aaliya's Books in Gemmayze, which is both the bane of her existence and the love of her life. If she can put the ills of Lebanon and the world aside for a moment, all she really longs for is more time to read and more time to write.

Perla Kantarjian

Perla Kantarjian is a Lebanese-Armenian writer, journalist, educator and editor, based in Beirut. Her work has appeared or is forthcoming in more than twenty-five publications, including *Epoch Press, Harpy Hybrid Review, NonBinary Review* and *International Literary Quarterly*. She is the former editor of Carpe Diem, *Annahar* newspaper's literary segment, and is currently a submissions reader for *Rusted Radishes*. She also writes for Bookstr, teaches literature at the International College, and copywrites for Black Lemon, an NFT Production House. She's also a letter-writing fanatic. Find her on @wordsbyperla

Rima Rantisi

Rima Rantisi teaches in the Department of English at the American University of Beirut and is the founding editor of *Rusted Radishes: Beirut Literary and Art Journal*. Her essays can be found in *Literary Hub, Assay: A Journal of Nonfiction*

Studies, Sweet: A Literary Confection, Past Ten, and *Slag Glass City.* She holds an MFA in creative nonfiction from the Vermont College of Fine Arts.

RL Attieh
RL Attieh is a text worker (writer, editor, occasional translator) currently based in Beirut. Her background in anthropology and literature, along with a developed practice in dance, are inseparable from her writing.

Samira Kaissi
Samira left Beirut at eighteen to pursue a career in science in the United States. After receiving a PhD from the University of Southern California, she had an adventurous career in academia and industry that took her from California to Lebanon to Ireland, where she now lives with her husband and daughter. She currently works with biotechnology start-ups. In 2020, she decided to finally dedicate more time to writing, her first passion. This is her first published story.

Sleiman El Hajj
Sleiman El Hajj is an assistant professor of creative and journalistic writing in the departments of English and communication arts at the Lebanese American University. Dr. El Hajj's output spans creative and critical research and has appeared in peer-reviewed journals, such as *Excursions, Life Writing,* and *Biography: An Interdisciplinary Quarterly.* He was appointed Visiting Research Fellow at the Department of International Development, University of Oxford, in 2019. His research interests include creative nonfiction, gender studies, narrative constructions of home, queer theory, and Middle Eastern literature.

Tala Arakji
By day, Tala is a strategist in advertising, where she offers her expertise in brand storytelling. By night, Tala is a writer with a passion for Arab narratives rooted in truth. Tala's writing is manifested in many forms: screenplays, podcasts, and opinion pieces. In 2020, Tala created a TV series that received funding but is still in the process of development.

Youmna Bou Hadir
Youmna is a Beirut-based author, content consultant, actress, and jazz singer who hopes to change the foundations of engagement and performance to include a real and intimate exchange between performer and audience member, writer, and reader through storytelling across media.

Zeina Saab
Zeina is a Lebanese American. In 2008, after receiving her MA in urban studies from MIT, she moved to Lebanon where she established The Nawaya Network, an NGO that provides individuals with access to income-generating opportunities through entrepreneurship, employment, and economic development programs. She is also the co-founder of SE Factory, a social enterprise that trains youth in software engineering and connects them with local and remote job opportunities.

Zena el Khalil
Author of *Beirut, I Love You*, Zena el Khalil is an artist and a sacred activist. Merging art and ritual, she creates exhibitions and ceremonies informed by yoga and shamanic practices. During the 2006 invasion of Lebanon, Zena's blog was published in the international press including the BBC, CNN, and *The Guardian*. She has been a speaker at the Nobel Peace Center in Oslo and holds a senior fellowship with TED. In 2017, Zena held a national-scale groundbreaking exhibition entitled "Sacred Catastrophe: Healing Lebanon" at the Beit Beirut museum.